BIOLOGY—OR OBLIVION

BIOLOGY— OR OBLIVION

Lessons from the Ultimate Science

by **Brian Hocking**, *1914-*
University of Alberta

SCHENKMAN PUBLISHING COMPANY, INC.
Cambridge, Massachusetts

Copyright © 1965
Schenkman Publishing Company, Inc.
Cambridge, Mass. 02138

A shorter and earlier version of this book,
The Ultimate Science, Copyright © by Brian Hocking

Printed in the United States of America.

Library of Congress Catalog Card Number: 65–20308

" . . . last scene of all,

That ends this strange eventful history,

Is second childishness and mere oblivion; . . . "

Shakespeare, *As You Like It*, II, vii.

Brian Hocking was born in London, England, in 1914. He was educated at North Ealing Boys School, London, and at Christ's Hospital, Horsham, Sussex. In 1933, he went to the Royal College of Science, where he studied a wide range of subjects, won the Murchison Medal for geology, and, in 1937, graduated B.Sc., with Honours, specializing in biology. Granted an Associateship of the Royal College of Science, he extended his range of science studies. In 1938, a senior appointment took him to India where he worked as a ferrous metallurgist for two years. This was followed by two years teaching school in India and a period of military service, during which he attained the rank of major, working on problems of stored-products entomology for the Southeast Asia Command. He came to Canada in 1946 to take up an appointment as Assistant Professor of Entomology at the University of Alberta. In 1948, he obtained his M.Sc. in entomology from that university; and, in 1953, his Ph.D. from the Faculty of Science, University of London. Dr. Hocking has been Professor of Entomology and Head of the Department at the University of Alberta since 1954. He has worked with insects in the Arctic and in many African countries as well as in the Far East. A member and a president of many scientific societies, he is the author of about a hundred papers on entomological and related topics.

FOREWORD

This book is written in the conviction that many of the problems
of life today would be solved if more people knew more about
life—more biology—earlier. It is designed to encourage this.

Conventional textbooks, to be sure, provide a plethora of
biological fact. Microfilm and computer can outdo both the
printer and the mind of man at this task and obscure all the
woods with trees. It is not for me to suggest a relationship between this and the persistence of a substrate for *Merulius lachry-
mans* in our academic biology (W. M. Wheeler, *Science*, Vol.
57),[1] but a need for something different—an escape if you wish,
from facts—has long been apparent. I have attempted to offer
this by dealing largely with issues, ideas, and principles—pungent,
picturesque, or adamantine—which the facts suggest. In doing so
I have been acutely conscious of the Charybdis of insufficient fact
and have thrown out accordingly a lifeline of references. This is
not, then,—there should be none such—a 'terminal course', unless
perhaps the first terminal, but should lead to further reading and
perhaps, for the favoured few caught in time, to an ultimate
career.

The book is based on the texts of eight half-hour radio lectures first broadcast in the Canadian Broadcasting Corporation
University of the Air series. The series was arranged by Lewis

[1]Wheeler titled his speech "The Dry-Rot of Our Academic Biology" (as
outgoing president of the American Society of Naturalists, 1922) since
some of his colleagues' activities so resembled the inroads of the fungus
Merulius lacrymans in old timber; he considered the possibility that a
conscientious librarian might catalogue his paper under cryptogamic
botany or phytopathology.

Miller, Ph.D., and produced by Peter Kappele, CBC Department of Public Affairs. I am indebted to these men for many helpful comments. My colleagues: George Ball, Ludwig von Bertalanffy, George Evans, Cleve Hickman, George Mackie, Ralph Nursall, and Clayton Person, each of whom read and commented on at least one chapter, deserve much of the credit for what may be good in the book. I am happy to accept full responsibility, however, for views expressed. My wife read or listened to all the chapters; more than once. It is a pleasure also to thank Judith Skeist of the Schenkman Publishing Company for her impeccable work in the final preparation of material for the printer.

I would like also to make specific acknowledgement as follows:
To her Majesty Queen Elizabeth II for her gracious permission to use reproductions of the Leonardo da Vinci drawings from the Royal Library at Windsor.
To Russell & Russell, Inc. Publishers, for permission to quote six lines from *The Roman Poet of Science, Lucretius: De Rerum Natura* by Carus Titus Lucretius, set in English verse by Alban Dewes Winspear, Harbor Scholars' Classics, New York, 1956.
To John Wiley & Sons, Inc., for permission to quote two brief passages from *Insect Pests of Farm, Garden, and Orchard* (5th ed.) by L. M. Peairs and R. H. Davidson, New York, 1956.
To the University of Chicago Press, for permission to quote a sentence from *The Fossil Evidence for Human Evolution: An Introduction to the Study of Palaeoanthropology* by W. E. Le Gros Clark, 'Copyright (1955) by the University of Chicago Press'.
To John Murray (Publishers) Limited, for permission to quote a short extract from *Success in Malaria Research* by Sir Ronald Ross.
To Putnam and Company Limited, for permission to include the quotation from *Seven Gothic Tales* by Isak Dinesen.
To David Higham Associated Limited (Authors' Agents), for permission to quote "The force that through the green fuse drives the flower" from the poems of Dylan Thomas.
To Mr. Ron Seward of the Department of Zoology, University of Alberta for a slide of *Amphiuma tridactylum Cuvier* red blood cells.

Illustrations from other sources are acknowledged in the captions.

Brian Hocking,
Edmonton, April 1965.

CONTENTS

. . . Picasso's dragon-fly.
Artists draw from the natural world.
(Courtesy: The National Gallery of Canada, Ottawa.)

1

SCARECROWS OF FOOLS

life among the sciences

Logical consequences
are the scarecrows of fools
and the beacons of wise men.
T. H. HUXLEY, *Science and Culture,* ix
*On the Hypothesis that Animals are
Automata.*

Karl Pearson referred to science as a classified index to the successive pages of sense impression, and in doing so he drew attention to the essentially verifiable nature of scientific knowledge (1). But to say that scientific knowledge is verifiable is not, by any means to equate science with truth, rather with a seeking after regularities of truth—or of probability—among the apparent chaotic diversity of phenomena in the universe we inhabit. Since the study of the senses falls properly within the sphere of biology, Karl Pearson's definition of science also serves as a pointer to the position of biology among the sciences. Thomas Henry Huxley (2) defined science as: "common sense . . . the necessary mode of working of the human mind", others have defined it as "horse sense; the sense which stops horses from betting on men". This last definition, flippant though it be, can also contribute to our understanding of science.

Science is a human activity, man a living organism subject to all biological laws; and man's least organic sciences and most inhuman humanities must all be colored by his organic nature.

Among the biological laws to which man has always been subject are those of natural selection, whereby those of us best fitted to our natural environment are selected by nature to live long enough to raise the next generation. Among the attributes of greatest importance to an animal in determining its fitness to its environment are its sense organs, and the "sense impressions" it receives from them: it is the classified index to these impressions which makes up science. Thomas Hobbes remarked 300 years ago that: "there is no conception in the mind of man that hath not at first been begotten upon the organs of sense"; man's special pride and joy, his mind, is largely an outcome of the selection of nature acting upon and through his sense organs.

When Huxley says then, that science is a "necessary mode of working of the human mind" he means just that. Those human minds of ages past which worked in any other way, were eliminated by natural selection. We may look, for an example in a familiar branch of physical science, to our arboreal ancestors, leaping from tree to tree. The brachiating apes can hardly be said to have anticipated Newton's discovery of the laws of gravity, but they must surely have had an intuitive perception of them. Their less perceptive relatives missed a leap, crashed, and failed to become our—and Newton's— ancestors. It was natural selection that discovered the laws of gravity. In more recent times, a

Figure 1.   **Arboreal ancestor.**

Figure 2. The long association which man has enjoyed with horses. Huxley to Marsh. (From *The Science of Life* by G. R. Taylor. Copyright © 1963 Thames and Hudson. Used by permission of McGraw-Hill Company.)

superior perception of relationships in plants and animals has had survival value for man both in allowing him to avoid poisonous plants and venomous animals, and, through intuitive chemistry, in permitting the preparation of toxins for use against still other animals for his food or clothing.

Doubtless a mutual appreciation of speed had something to do with the long association which man has enjoyed with horses. Perhaps this association in part explains the scientific nature of horse sense and our superior knowledge of the evolution of this animal. It is the fact that science deals with calculated probabilities as well as with truth that introduces, as we shall see, as big an element of chance into the ultimate science as can be found on any race track. From conception to decay nature tosses coins for us.

We must conclude from all this that children of today have, selected within them, the elements of much of our basic fabric of scientific law and principle. If our science teachers would but realise this and draw on it, instead of burying it under meaningless trivialities of contemporary technology, how much easier their task would be; and how much happier their charges. Much of what is taught today in the name of science is but temporary applications of scientific knowledge, often already familiar to the recipient from his daily living experience; often obsolete before graduation.

Science deals with material things, our perceptions of them, the laws they obey, and the orderly relationships between them. It cannot well be taught from books and charts and pictures, which carry but second-hand knowledge, but must be taught by the manipulation of material things themselves. It is not for nothing that *experience* and *experiment* have the same derivation. Any child who has not had his native curiosity negated out of him by over anxious parents—and teachers, will learn science spontaneously. He needs only to be placed in an appropriate environment of material things—especially living ones—and provided with the appropriate aids to his senses—rules, balances, and timers; thermometers, lenses, and microscopes, and such tools of the trade as containers and burners, wire and batteries, string and sealing-wax. The task of the teacher is but to provide these and a modicum of guidance.

Scientific information is growing explosively. More than 60,000 scientific periodicals—weeklies, monthlies, or quarterlies, are now being published; few libraries handle more than a small percentage of these. The rate at which information is produced has doubled in the last 25 years and is likely to double again in the next. It follows that a teacher who thought he had completed his training in 1945 is faced with the problem of mastering nearly as much new material produced since that time as was then available to him, accumulated since science began. Obviously he cannot do it and still find time to teach. Fortunately much of this new material is applied and ephemeral and teachers of younger people would do well to leave this alone. Much of it is available in the more concentrated form of reviews, but some reference to original material remains necessary. There is some truth in the exaggerated statement that it takes 20 years to get new information into the textbooks, and 50 years to get it out again, when it proves to be wrong.

While this explosive growth of science and scientists continues— ninety per cent of all scientists are alive today—every scientist needs to concern himself with science education, both as a legacy to the next generation of scientists, and that his pronouncements do not fall on the stony ground of an uncomprehending public.

Although it is much more difficult for anybody to cover these vast fields today, it is much more important that somebody should do so. Some people at least must straddle the gaps between the physical sciences and the life sciences, the life sciences and the earth sciences, between chemistry and astronomy, taxonomy and atomic physics. This alone will give coherence to the whole. Faced with the expanse of modern scientific knowledge and its fantastically accelerating rate of growth, it is all too easy for the small mind to restrict itself to a smaller and smaller specialization. All too easy for wisdom, to be drowned in knowledge.

Whether or not the science teacher needs to master this increasingly vast bulk of knowledge, it exists and will influence

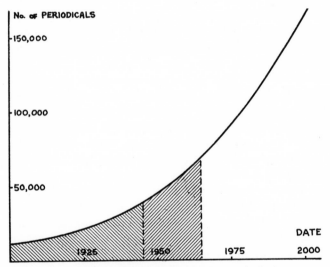

Figure 3.   Scientific information is growing explosively.

human life profoundly in years to come (3). The wisdom with which it is used will not, in the main, depend on the scientists who are making it—they are unlikely ever to have a majority vote in a democracy, and few have any personal interest in dictatorships. It will depend on the general public. Our future then, if we are to have one, depends on a broad and balanced understanding of science, its methods and principles, and what it can and cannot do, by the next generation as a whole. This is to say it depends on science teachers today, especially at the junior levels. I say 'if we are to have one' because already there are troubles ahead on three fronts, the physical threat of atomic radiation and explosion, the chemical threat of toxic contamination and pollution, and the biological threats of other human activities to the survival of many organisms and eventually of man himself; not to mention the direct threat of his own population. But the scientist is no more to blame for this than anybody else, unless he fails to concern himself about education. His search for knowledge is for its own sake. The use to which his findings are put is the concern of administrators and technologists, business men, advertisers, and consumers. The scientist could not control it if he would.

Even today it is still possible, and indeed customary, for a biologist to receive substantial training in the physical sciences which are basic to biology. But it is rare for people trained in the physical sciences to have similar training in biology. Throughout history, many of the significant leaps of progress in science have come from men with an unusual combination of interests. Leeuwenhoek in biology, Galileo in physics and Boyle in chemistry, showed this hybrid vigor as we may call it, this mutual fertilization of ideas. This is just one reason why those trained in the physical sciences should acquire some familiarity with biology. The ultimate purposes of the physical sciences must be in biology for science is human knowledge, and man is alive still.

Much has been made of the methods of science in attempts to define it, and its pedestrian progress by hypothesis and experiment is indeed one of its characteristics. But more important than its methods is the accumulated law and principle which these methods have produced over the centuries.

Of course there is still much that is conflicting in the literature of the sciences, and perhaps especially in the science of life. But conflict on any matter that properly falls within the realm of science can be ultimately resolved by experiment. In fact the progress of science results largely from the referring back of conflicts to the test of experiment, while matters beyond the realm of science cannot be so decided, but must be accepted, or rejected, on faith.

Now while conflict and experiment account for the pedestrian progress of science, the spur which at intervals gives wings to these processes is the brilliant hypothesis, the inspired idea. These flashes of genius seem to result from a happy combination of a fertile and receptive mind and appropriately suggestive circumstances. For many such, divine inspiration has been claimed as when Sir Ronald Ross, after elucidating the transmission of malaria wrote:

"This day relenting God
Hath placed within my hand
"A wondrous thing . . ."

For others it might well have been, as when the principle of natural selection occurred to Alfred Russell Wallace, while sweating out an attack of this same fever, or the ring structure of benzene to August Kekulé in a dream of snakes chasing their own tails. A few would be more appropriately ascribed to the devil. Good or bad, they become immediate targets of experimental test. "Let us learn to dream, gentlemen," said Kekulé, "then perhaps we shall find the truth . . . but let us beware of publishing our dreams before they have been put to the proof of the waking understanding."

Brilliant hypotheses are in no way dependent on the scientific method, although scientific progress may depend on them. They are exactly comparable to inspiration in the arts; it is significant that Kekulé started life as an architect, perhaps too that Wallace took ultimate refuge in spiritualism. We can hardly claim yet, that we can educate for inspiration; but the education of a scientist must at least leave room for this.

How to handle this arduous, onerous task in education? As I have said already, given a chance science and evolution will handle it for us—but the chance must be given generously. While there are signs of niggardly movement towards this, North America, for all its high standard of living or perhaps because of a complacency this engenders, has a long way to go. The new world still has a lot to learn from the old both in the provision of the environment for the learning of science, and in the methods of

Figure 4. The classroom must be expanded to nature's laboratory out-
doors.

teaching it. It is an ill wind that blows no good and perhaps the
flood of knowledge will enforce a long overdue reassessment of
the place in education of the relatively changeless aspects of science—its history (4) and its principles.

The environment must contain, as well as the tools of science,
the materials to use them on, both inorganic and organic, the
living and the dead. No room in which science is taught should
be without its living plants and animals, aquatic and terrestrial,
native and exotic, they should fill the windows and line the walls.
And when they die they must be preserved to build a permanent
museum of teaching material. The liveliest of teachers is handi-
capped with naught but dead materials. Not only must a teacher—
and a class—bring living material into the classroom, but class
and teacher must get together in the field, despite all obstacles.
If there is an excuse for our shortage of well equipped school
laboratories it is that many of us have nature's great laboratory
at our doorsteps. North America's history is short enough that the
humblest high school science class can hope to discover something
new in this laboratory, and thus experience a taste of the supreme
thrill of scientific work than which nothing can be more stimulat-
ing. Such things ring the bell of history; we cannot afford to
leave them silent.

I have been speaking of the teaching, not only of biology, but of science. To delineate precisely the physical sciences, the earth sciences and the life sciences; or physics, chemistry, and biology, is impossible and should remain so. Drawing dividing lines is the preoccupation of minds incapable of building bridges. It may be foolish of me to trespass into other fields in a book on biology; it is a folly I am content to be accused of. It is important, despite the formal breakdown into physics, chemistry, and biology, that the essential unity of the sciences, and even their affinities with the arts and humanities, be in some way conveyed to the student. One of the more hopeful signs for the future is the extent to which this is happening, and the extent to which the techniques and resources of the physical sciences are being applied to problems in the life sciences. As we live, this must be so; A. N. Whitehead remarked somewhat hopefully, many years ago, that science is becoming the study of organisms (5). Biology is the ultimate science in two senses: its study follows naturally on that of physics, chemistry, and the earth sciences, and no other major branch of science follows on from it.

I have tried in the following chapters, to tell something of the story of living things as we know it today in what seems to me a logical sequence: I start with the origin of life, then the structure of plants and animals, the way in which they have changed, and how all this is reflected in the way we classify them today. Then from this I go into the way in which they operate, firstly within themselves, and then in relation to each other and their surroundings. Finally I have tried to assess man's relationship to other organisms, to see what lessons we can learn from this to guide our future activities, and to develop what I might call a biologists' creed.

My account is inevitably biased by personal interests and experiences. It would be dull were it otherwise. Such a short account inevitably contains many statements which should be qualified; qualifying material will be found in most of the references at the end of the book.

I would like to close this chapter by quoting once more from one of the greatest contributors to science education, T. H. Huxley, whose definition of science we started out with and whose common sense came very close to horse sense. "Logical consequences", said Huxley "are the scarecrows of fools and the beacons of wise men". Science deals with logical consequences; the world of the next generation will be in no small measure a logical consequence of the science we teach to it now.

2

IN
THE
BEGINNING

the origins
of life

In the beginning . . .
. . .the earth was void and empty . . .
Genesis i. 1

Biology is the study of life, of all that this involves, from the life that you and I live to that elusive quality that distinguishes a fresh and fertile egg from a boiled one, a germinating seed from popcorn, a tree from a log, a man from his corpse. But, in the present state of our science, in order to study this elusive thing, we have to study plants and animals, the organisms that manifest it, or, alas too frequently, for reasons of convenience, the dead and usually distorted remains of these. Many people find these studies satisfying in themselves, as indeed they are. But I think most serious biologists are really concerned too with the nature of life itself; and even in their simplest studies of the most familiar organisms, they are looking towards this.

Let us look, for a moment, then, at the things that distinguish a living organism from a dead one and from other objects, since these obviously come close to the nature of life. The first characteristic of every living thing is that it has come from other living things similar to, but not the same as, itself. This vitally important qualification—not the same as—is often omitted from statements of this characteristic. Most living things are also capable of producing, or—as biologists say—reproducing, other living things also similar to themselves. This presupposes a second important characteristic of living things: the ability to grow or increase in size, since otherwise no object can repeatedly give rise to other objects as big as itself. And along with this increase in size comes an increase in complexity.

A third characteristic of living things is that of responding or reacting to a stimulus. Here, already, we come up against the dependence of biology on physics and chemistry; for a stimulus is nothing more or less than a physical or chemical change or condition impinging upon the organism. This responsiveness is usually taken to apply only to the individual: a plant, the shoots of which grow upwards and the roots downwards under the stimulus of gravity; or an animal, which will usually recoil or retreat from an electrical stimulus or from extremes of temperature. It is not restricted to living things; a lamp will respond to an electrical stimulus by shining; automata can be built that will react in an animal-like manner to many stimuli. The famous mechanical tortoise of Dr. Walter, *Machina speculatrix*, even responded to "hunger"—an exhausted battery—by returning to base for recharging.

But responsiveness is also a feature, and I think more especially so, of species, which for the moment we may define as the entire populations of particular kinds of plants and animals. Now the response of a species to the collective stimuli of its surroundings is, of course, to change in successive generations, or—as biologists say—evolve, in a direction determined by the nature of these surroundings. I shall deal more fully with this key process of biology later. The distinction between the response of an individual and that of a species is of particular importance because while the individual response may readily be imitated in physical and chemical systems, the species response may not. If we define evolution as the response of a species to the collective stimuli of its environment, then this becomes a much more rigid criterion of life than the response of an individual to a stimulus. One of the best-documented examples of this process is to be found in the horse, a surviving line from small, short-legged four-toed ancestors of sixty million years ago. Fleetness of foot has increased under the stimulus of high-speed predators. Documentation of a parallel process in man's ancestry, the increase of brain size and intelligence from those of the apes, is steadily accumulating (1).

When the world began, four or five billion years ago, it was dead. Nothing on it lived. There was then no life to study and of

12

course nobody to study it—no biology. Physics and chemistry flourished—or at least the processes of them did. Days were short. The air was without oxygen. It was hot, and sunlight was very different then from now: ultra-violet was intense; that is, you could have acquired a tan in very short order—if you did not roast first.

Perhaps two-thirds of the time from then till now, a billion and a half years ago, the first strange living processes began; biology became possible. In view of what I have said about the characteristics of living things, it is appropriate to suggest that the infant life was the offspring of a marriage between chemical and physical conditions. Chemically, hydrogen, nitrogen, methane, and other simple carbon compounds, were plentiful, but oxygen was only present in combined form, as in water. Physically, energy was abundant in the radiant heat and the ultra-violet of sunlight, and perhaps in electrical discharges. In the seas of these primeval times, perhaps near the shores where more complex compounds could have been adsorbed onto clays and concentrated, life was conceived.

This, of course, is guesswork; but guided guesses—hypotheses— are the first rungs of the ladder of science, becoming theories as the harder factual sides of the ladder are extended, and finally facts when the ladder makes firm contact with structures established by other ladders of hypothesis. Some stages of these processes in the formation of living matter will occur so readily that they can be reproduced in the laboratory. In the last ten or twenty years, more and more exciting discoveries in biology have lent support to these views of what took place on the earth millions of years ago (2).

But we cannot easily grasp time of this magnitude. We read in the Bible, in the first chapter of Genesis, that the earth was made in six days, living things being produced on three of these; but there are many examples of the elasticity of biblical time. St. Augustine held that creation actually took place in a single instant but that the six day idea was introduced to make the events easier to grasp. With equal validity we may perhaps translate what most authorities now believe to have occupied about five billion years into the familiar scale of a single year. This is the same factor of change as St. Augustine's, if we assume 'instant' to have been one ten-thousandth of a second (100 microsec.). Let us contract the whole existence of the world, then, into a single year. The world began on January 1st. Then conditions in which life could have arisen developed perhaps early in August. The oldest known fossils, life of the past imprinted in the rocks, were living things about mid October; and life was abundant, both plants and animals, most of them in the seas, by the end of that month. In mid December, dinosaurs and other reptiles dominated the scene. Mammals, with hairy covering and suckling their young, only appeared in time for Christmas; and on New Year's eve, at about five minutes to midnight, from amongst them stumbled man. Of these five minutes of man's existence, recorded history represents about the time the clock takes to strike twelve.

On the last stroke of twelve, back in the seventeenth century, the French philosopher René Descartes, speaking of branches of mathematics, said 'all the phenomena of nature may be explained by their means'; and for Descartes, nature included physics and chemistry as well as biology. In this view he was largely influenced by the great Belgian anatomist Vesalius, and by William Harvey's recently published mechanical explanation of the circulation of the blood. In the succeeding centuries bitter controversy followed on a similar point: was life explicable in terms of physics and chemistry? The mechanists, who thought it was, opposed the vitalists who denied this. While our knowledge of physics and chemistry and biology is today much more extensive, it is not yet deep enough to give a certain answer to this question, and perhaps it never will be. On the other hand, no phenomenon outside of these two sciences has yet been demonstrated in living things, by metaphysicians or by scientists.

Although evolution is often thought of as a purely biological concept, in the light of these controversies we would do well to look upon it as a continuous process through physics and chemistry into biology; and on through this into we know not what. It is a process of progressively increasing complexity of structure; in this modern view, firstly of atoms into molecules, later of molecules into supermolecules, such as polymers and proteins, and later again, of these bricks into primitive organisms, which again progressively increase in complexity.

Man likes to regard himself as the culmination of this process

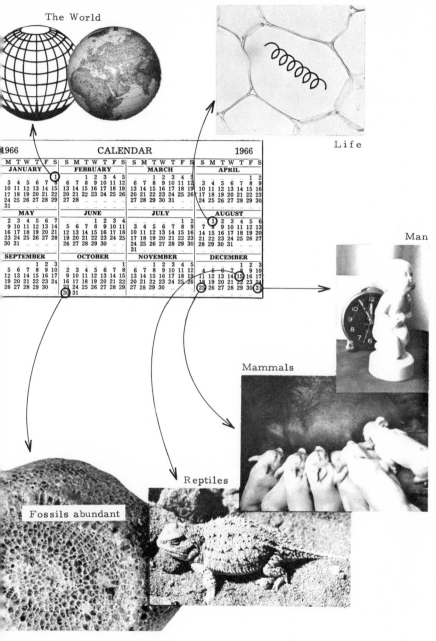

Figure 5. The World began on January 1st . . . the time scale reduced to one five billionth.

of evolution. Indeed, some modern biological thinkers seem to doubt whether man is correctly included in the science of life at all and consider humanity to be on a different plane from other organisms (3, 4). This would make the study of man a new science for which we may coin the term 'neosymbology', since the proponents of this view emphasize the use of symbols as man's distinguishing characteristic. If this proves correct, then biology may no longer be referred to as the ultimate science. It seems to me likely, however, that most animal species see themselves as the centre of things and the purpose of creation, certainly those that are, like man, extremely specialized. (We may surmise for example that the last thoughts to simmer in the thick head of *Tyrannosaurus rex*—one of the largest of the dinosaurs—before it floundered into fossil oblivion, concerned the inferiority of all beasts of smaller size. As subjects for biological study we have no reason to differentiate between man and *Tyrannosaurus*.)

The thread of evolution is inextricably woven through the whole of biology. Let us take a closer look at the threadlike beginnings of this story. I have mentioned the supermolecules, polymers and proteins, as the final pre-living stages.

Polymers are molecules of many parts, each alike and associated together. In proteins, the parts within the molecule differ, so that a much greater variety of them is possible. Both polymers and proteins have usually a threadlike structure. How did these things acquire the characteristics that made them alive?

Working downwards in size from the cell, we find in all but the most primitive cells a more or less ovoid control centre, the nucleus, and within the nucleus more threadlike structures, the chromosomes. These 'coloured bodies' are so called because they were first revealed by the very useful biological technique of staining, applied to cells in the process of dividing. Many stains or dyes are picked up much more strongly by the chromosomes than by other parts of the cell. Smaller than the chromosomes of the cells of plants and animals, but larger than most protein molecules, are the strange and remarkable molecules of the desoxyribosenucleic acids, keys to inheritance, that biologists nearly always refer to as D.N.A.—Desoxyribose Nucleic Acid. We can well describe DNA as 'such stuff as genes are made on', and many thousands of genes go to make a chromosome.

The molecules of DNA can be likened to a cross between a zipper and a corkscrew. Take a zipper ten feet long and wind it around a half inch curtain rod. Extract the rod and you will have something like the double helix of a DNA molecule magnified some five million times. The tapes of the zipper holding the teeth

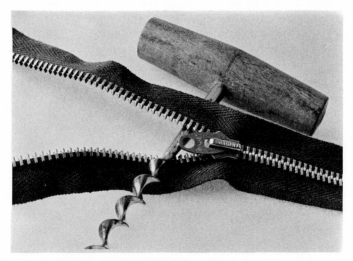

Figure 6.   DNA . . . a cross between a zipper and a corkscrew.

Figure 7.   The double helix of a DNA molecule.

together on either side, are regular alternations of molecules of a sugar and of phosphoric acid. The teeth of the zipper are nitrogen bases, subsidiary molecules of a kind which could well have been formed initially in the marriage between physical and chemical conditions in the seas of the primeval earth. These subsidiary molecules are of four kinds only: A, B, C, and D, and they hook together by hydrogen bonds. But only two combinations are possible: A with C, and B with D. In all other respects any arrangement by sequence or by side of the zipper may occur. Attach to the tapes of this zipper a variety of protein molecules and you have a model of a gene, much magnified of course. A thousand or so such genes make up a chromosome and every plant and animal species has a fixed and characteristic number of chromosomes in each cell.

It will perhaps be easier to grasp these ideas if we change our size scale throughout as we did our time scale. Here we need a more modest change, say one to ten thousand or about a foot to two miles, one 500-thousandth of that which we used in time. Let us then magnify a very large protein molecule or a small gene or a virus—an organism on the borderland of the living—some ten thousand times to make it just visible to the naked eye, say one tenth of a millimetre across, about the size of a grain of salt. A large virus, a bacterium, or a chromosome, might now be as big as a grain of rice, a red blood cell like a small saucer, and the largest cell as big as a skating rink. A man on this scale would tower above Mount Everest and the top of a giant redwood felled in California would provide roosts for the gull and the eagle in Salt Lake City, Utah.

So much for the structure of DNA, this near magic material; what of its function? There may be several feet of DNA in a cell and as many as 3,000 units in a DNA molecule, and every different arrangement of the four nitrogen bases is a different material. This means that a tremendous variety of DNA molecules is possible. Then there are innumerable different protein molecules from which those attached to the side tapes may be chosen, and innumerable sequences in which, once chosen, they may be arranged. So that the number of different genes that is possible begins to stagger the imagination. Since genes are the bases of organisms, one begins to marvel not at the diversity of living

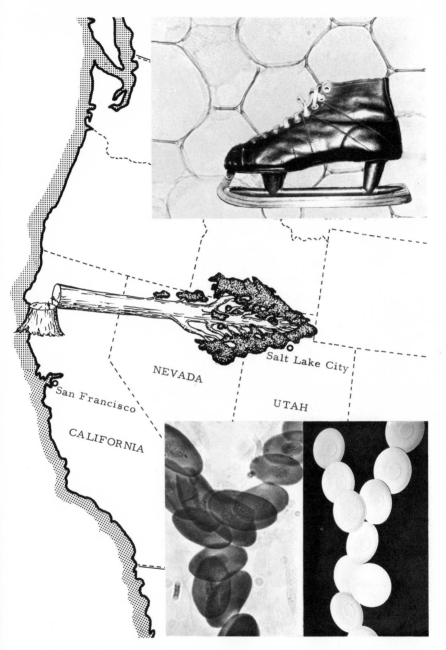

Figure 8. The size scale, times ten thousand; a large cell becomes a skating rink, a redwood reaches Salt Lake City, a red blood cell becomes a saucer.

things, but at their similarity, and their restriction to a rather small number of basic structural designs.

Now DNA molecules, like zippers, can be readily separated into two halves. We know little of how this happens, and less still of how it first happened. Once the two halves have been separated, in a suitable chemical medium each half could manufacture a replacement for the other half it had lost by picking up the appropriate submolecules, the four nitrogen bases—so to speak, by their zipper teeth—from the medium around it, following these by the tapes. We should then have two identical genes instead of one. This is both reproduction, our first characteristic of life, and also, linked with this, the second characteristic, growth.

Among the protein molecules attached on the tape will be found those peculiar ones known as enzymes, which can, by some facile liaison with the raw material, accelerate chemical changes while remaining unchanged themselves. Through such agencies as these the gene controls the happenings around it, and, perhaps collectively in this way, the genes co-operate in the chromosomes of the nucleus to acquire or fabricate the remaining components of all cells. These are a rather clear, non-uniform, viscous fluid, the cytoplasm, and its inclusions and enveloping membranes. Once these lifelike materials had been formed, the physical forces between the molecules, and between them and the water surrounding them, led to patterns of arrangement that finally culminated in the first living cells, the units of which all organisms are built. These same forces result in movements—responses to chemical and physical stimuli—our third characteristic of life, at the level of the individual organism.

Those genes that do this best in the prevailing environment, that is genes with arrangements of zipper teeth most readily matched, will multiply at the expense of others; and we have this characteristic at the species level—evolution.

Now although the chance that molecules and environment should occur in the combination required for life to begin at any given time and place in nature is incredibly small, the space and the time that have been available for these things to happen in are incredibly large, so that the net chance is reasonable. It has been well said, in this connection, that if a monkey were to sit at a typewriter and type at random, given everlasting life, he would eventually type the complete works of William Shakespeare.

Now these first organisms were very small; but they must have multiplied very rapidly, and the suspensions of organic material in favourable parts of the seas in which they developed must have become depleted as they multiplied—like man today, they too had a population problem. In these circumstances, an organism that could manufacture some of its requirement of organic nutrients for itself from readily available materials would have had a tremendous advantage. But such a process needs energy; sunlight was the most readily available source. Such an organism was formed; genes that could make photosynthetic pigments, capable of absorbing energy from sunlight to build organic compounds, did arise in the forerunners of plants. They were improved by selection in the algae of the seas, and in some such way as this the familiar green chlorophyll of today's plants was invented.

Figure 9. Probability of typing the works of Shakespeare.

Now in the process of photosynthesis, not only is the energy of sunlight stored in chemical form as sugars and starch, but also oxygen is produced; so gradually the air began to approach its present-day composition, with enough oxygen to support life on dry land. Changes in the composition of the air reduced the intensity of ultra-violet at the earth's surface, and allowed life to emerge from the protective screen of the sea and adapt to conditions on the land. We have seen that competition for food and space in the sea had been getting severe. On land the interaction between the weather and the rocks had produced something resembling soil. Plants assisted this process and grew upwards, in competition with each other for sunlight. Then the insects, from these elevated perches, invaded the air, the last vast habitat, and life was everywhere.

As plant growth spread and built up reserves of energy-rich organic materials, the stage was set for the expansion of this new terrestrial life. The animals on this stage ate the plants and used the plant-produced oxygen to obtain energy from the organic materials in them. They were eaten in turn by other animals, such as you and me, which also used plant-produced oxygen. How the plants must despise us animals—doubly dependent on these green philanthropists of the living world!

Not only do most biologists believe that life originated in the way I have described, but also there is much and growing evidence, based chiefly on differences in the biochemistry of various groups of organisms, that this has occurred more than once on this planet and perhaps on many others. This does not alter the fact that from the short-term viewpoint of a human life, or even perhaps of man's tenure of this planet, living things are not normally generated spontaneously. When Pasteur showed this with his elegant flasks of boiled broth in 1864 he was as right as he could be in the time at his disposal. Strict proof that something never happens is impossible.

This brings us to an aspect of life that is often overlooked, namely its relationship to time—not geological time now, but that of everyday life. When we examine a dead preserved plant or animal we are in fact seeing only a cross-section of the organism in time. Organisms have a span of life from fertilization of an egg by a spermatozoon or a seed by a pollen nucleus to final death and decay. It is important to remember this, and to remember too that although the final form of an animal is influenced by the surroundings or environment in which it develops, nevertheless the general features of the kind or species, and indeed most of the special features of the individual, are determined by material, the genes, within the nuclei of the parent cells. These cells, ova and spermatozoa or gametes, are themselves only distinguishable as individuals by special and elaborate techniques, and it is often difficult to distinguish between those of different species or even of

22

different families. The manner in which this minute amount of material determines the precise and specific form of the many tons of a whale or an elephant is known as morphogenesis, the development of form. That the minute and similar germ cells of animals so different as a man and a mayfly always turn out right has long been a puzzle. This led in the seventeenth century to the imaginings of homunculi, or little men, rolled up inside human spermatozoa. Leonardo da Vinci recorded the then traditional view that the male transferred the soul or 'animal spirit' to the female at mating as well as the sperm. This was reputed to come from the spinal cord (5). Aristotle, considering this problem much earlier still, concluded that the female cell, the ovum, contributed the substance and the male cell the form of the new individual.

Figure 10. Fossils . . . borderline between living and nonliving things.

We have seen how living things differ from non-living things and how uncertain the borderline between these is. We have seen how biologists think these differences first arose, and should perhaps repeat here that much of this is speculative and is likely to remain so for some time to come. We have seen too the role of chance in these processes; and this is no speculation, as will be abundantly clear when we come on to discuss genetics. King Chance, challenged only by the parliament of the environment and its collective stimuli, has ruled over the subsequent course of evolution of plants and animals. It has been a long rule, and, when we contemplate the diverse beauty of form and colour and song and scent and texture in the living world, I think we may say a distinguished one, from these one or more initial occurrences up to and including the origin and the subsequent development of man.

A proper study of mankind is certainly man, and, if you wish, the humanities he produces. But how much more proper this study becomes when it is set in the context of the fellow beings with which man shares this world and based on an excursion back into geological time, through the fascinating kaleidoscope of what has gone before.

3

BRICKS
ARE
ALIVE

the structure
of living things

Sir, he made a chimney in my father's
house, and the bricks are alive at
this day to testify it . . .
SHAKESPEARE, *King Henry VI,
Part II,* IV, ii

It is one of the most unfortunate facts in biology that the structure of plants and animals, the manner in which they have
developed and are put together, can be most easily studied by
cutting them apart, by dissection. This has two drawbacks: firstly,
it means that a destructive process must be used in an attempt to
understand an integrative and progressive one; secondly, the essential living quality of an organism is usually destroyed before its
acquaintance can be made.

The process of examination is sometimes so exacting that the
end may be lost sight of in preoccupation with the means. So
much so that even the name of the means has come to be sub-
stituted for the end. Anatomy originally meant cutting apart—the
same in Greek as a word of Latin origin, dissection; but it is now
used to refer to the study of structure itself, the objective of this
process.

The original concept of the atom, the basic unit of the chemist,
was as the smallest part into which matter could be cut; the word
'atom', of common origin with anatomy, means uncuttable. The
biological equivalent, that which cannot be further divided and
retain its living identity, is the cell. Buildings are made of bricks
and organisms are made of cells. But a cell differs from a brick
in two important ways: firstly, it can grow and become two cells;
secondly, the cells it gives rise to can develop in different ways or
differentiate—they may become not only the bricks of the body

but also the mortar, the beams and boards and joists, the shingles, the wiring, and the plumbing. And through all this, a few of them remain unchanged, able to set out on their own under suitable conditions, and, in their turn, multiply and differentiate into a new organism, built of new bricks. This is reproduction.

Since the recognition of the importance of the cell as the biological unit of structure, a new discipline, histology, the study of cells and tissues has grown up. The most widely used technique is to kill and fix or preserve the tissues and then slice them into sections a small fraction of a millimetre in thickness. Such sections are usually treated with one or more stains to show up particular components. We have seen that this differential affinity for stains led to the name chromosome, meaning 'coloured body', for the threadlike carriers of inheritance. Sections are mounted on glass for microscopic examination or, more recently, prepared in various ways for the electron microscope. For many years there was a big gap in the size scale between the smallest objects which could be examined with the light microscope, not much less than a thousandth of a millimetre, and the largest which could be studied by the methods of particle physics, about a millionth of a millimetre, or one thousand times smaller. This gap spans the borderland of the living; viruses, cell components, and macromolecules are all within it. For this reason, the development of the electron microscope, which allows objects of this size to be studied through their effects on a magnetically focussed stream of electrons, has been of great importance in biology. The most striking revelation by this technique has been the widespread occurrence in living matter of an intricate inter-leaving of membranes, appearing in photographs of thin sections of course as series of more or less parallel lines (1). The surface area of a cell dwindles to insignificance beside the surfaces available for chemical exchange within it. The significance of the accumulated information about the finer structure of cells in relation to the living processes, however, needs to be interpreted carefully.

Let us then take another look at the general features of the cell, this remarkable living brick. Despite its differences from a brick, it very often has one important resemblance: its shape or form. This similarity in form is no indication of relationship. Man invented bricks before he discovered cells; nature evolved cells without reference to man. But neither is it accidental. Both brick and cell take different forms, but both are very frequently rectangular with different dimensions in all three axes. Such a shape lends itself most readily to the construction of walls—or of organisms—with a variety of dimensions and proportions. Another cell shape of wide general usefulness is a regular polyhedron. The bubbles within a mass of foam have this shape, with their many similar geometrical faces. It can provide the simplest symmetrical filling of a space with the maximum strength for the amount of material used. This cell form is found in the early embryos of most animals and in the roots and stems of plants. It is found, too, as a storage tissue in both plants and animals, since it can also provide the maximum capacity for the amount of building material used. The base of a cell of a honeycomb has nearly the same form (2). Architects and engineers are only now beginning to appreciate the possibilities of these polyhedral shapes; the honeybee used them before man was thought of.

The simplest shape for a cell is a sphere, and many eggs and single-celled organisms such as bacteria and protozoa have this shape; so of course does a single bubble. The reason for this is that a sphere has the minimum surface area for a given volume, so that surface tension tends to pull a cell into this shape. In opposition to surface tension is the pressure set up within the cell by the water drawn into it by the solutions it contains. This process of osmosis, which keeps a cell inflated with fluid by osmotic pressure, is very important to the cell. Osmosis and surface tension argue out the final shape of the cell with the biological demands that may be made upon it. Its final shape is a compromise. A red blood cell has to be rounded to pass readily through the small tubular capillaries and must have a large surface area to absorb oxygen, so it is plate-like. The stem of a plant requires linear strength and among its cells are long, narrow fibres.

These and other modified cells, then, make up the tissues of the plant and the animal. The tissues make up the organs, and the tissues and organs make up the body. Aristotle (3) with his delightful directness, expressed the distinction between tissues and organs in the opening sentence of his *Historia Animalium* as follows:

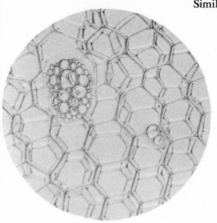

Figure 11. Bubbles within a mass of foam

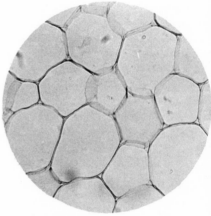

Figure 12. Cells from a plant stem.

Figure 13. Foundation of cells of honeycomb.

Some parts of animals are simple, and these can be divided into like parts, as flesh into pieces of flesh; others are compound, and cannot be divided into like parts, as the hand cannot be divided into hands, nor the face into faces. All the compound parts also are made up of simple parts—the hand, for example, of flesh and sinew and bone.

But Aristotle, of course, knew nothing of cells, the discovery of which had to await the microscope. Indeed, apart from the contributions of Aristotle's successors (Theophrastus on the structure of plants and Galen on human structure) some fifteen hundred years had to pass before lesser men, aided by the microscope, made significant additions to the knowledge that Aristotle had of the structure of living things.

The way back from the dark ages into a scientific approach to anatomy was led by a trio of famous artists. Firstly, Botticelli of Florence, whose famous picture *Primavera* contains no less than thirty different plants drawn from life and recognizable as to species. Secondly, Leonardo da Vinci, almost a neighbour of his, who drew and painted the structure and studied the functions of many animals. Thirdly, Albrecht Dürer of Nuremberg, the inventor of etching, who used this process and the woodcut to illustrate many plants and animals from life and whose widow published in 1528 his Treatise on Human Proportion.

Of course, in the dark ages between Aristotle and Leonardo da Vinci, some knowledge was kept alive in the copyings of the writings of Aristotle and his contemporaries. These and other handwritten books, in necessarily small numbers, tell a pathetic tale of the blind acceptance of tradition and hearsay. In the bestiaries and herbals—illustrated natural histories, originally in Latin but translated into many languages—are to be found the most improbable descriptions of the structure even of familiar animals and plants. Yet, though we laugh at them today, nature is full of improbable things and many a germ of truth was preserved in the bestiaries. Strangely enough, it seems that some knowledge was preserved too in unwritten form in the experience of many butchers and cooks and woodsmen in whom a spark of scientific inquisitiveness occurred.

Throughout these earlier periods, even after the Dark Ages, man took an overriding interest in his own structure. The practice of dissecting other animals was viewed as contemptible and few anatomists would admit to it. But even the great Vesalius prac-

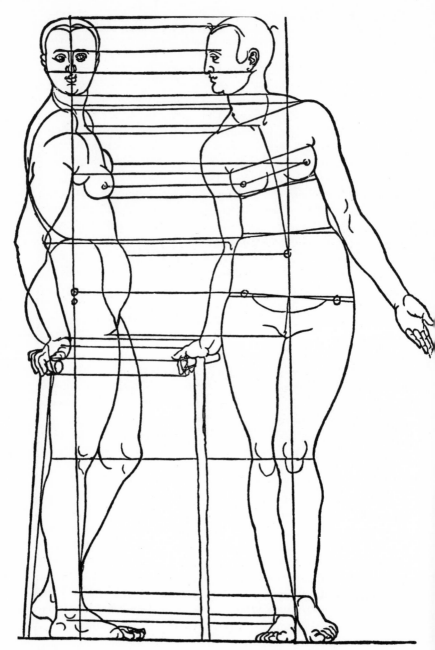

Figure 14. From Albrecht Durer's "Treatise on human proportion".

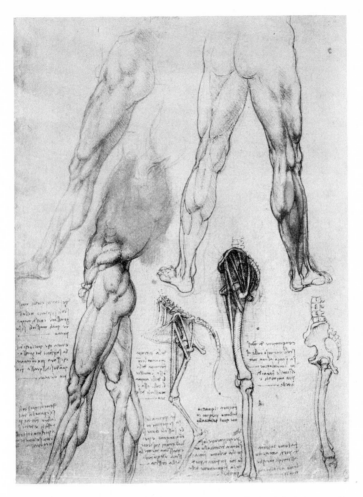

Figure 15. Leonardo da Vinci's comparison of the hind leg of horse and man . . . one of the earliest comparative studies.

tised it when convenient. He realized, as some others did, that what was obscure in man might be clear in another animal. Some of the illustrations in his major work, *De Humani Corporis Fabrica* have since been found to have been drawn from animals other than man (4).

Robert Hooke (5) in 1665, with the newly invented microscope, was perhaps the first to recognize the cellular structure of
plants. In his *Micrographia* he describes his examination of the
cell walls in cork, rather polyhedral ones, in these words:

> I . . . cut off from the former smooth surface an exceeding thin piece
> of it, and placing it on a black object plate . . . and casting the light
> on it with a deep plano-convex glass, I could exceedingly plainly per-
> ceive it to be all perforated and porous, much like a honeycomb . . .

But it was not until the nineteenth century that Schleiden, for
plants, and Schwann, for animals, explicitly established the role
of the cell as the essential unit of structure in living things.

The size of cells as well as their shape is limited by natural
laws. The needs of a cell are determined as to quantity by its
bulk, but the rate at which it can obtain these is determined by
the extent of its surface membrane. Everything going into or out
of a cell must pass through the surface membrane, which must
therefore have a certain area in relation to the bulk or weight
of the cell. But the bigger anything is, the less surface it has in
relation to its bulk. If you doubt this, go and buy a dozen oranges
and try to wrap them individually in the paper of the bag they
came in! So there is a maximum size for a cell of a given shape,
the size at which there is just sufficient surface membrane to
supply the needs of the matter it contains. This principle often
influences the shape of cells as well as setting limits to their size.
Similar considerations play a part in determining the inner structure of cells since the nucleus, the core of the cell, controls its
activities by the passage of materials through its own surface
membrane. So there must also be a fairly constant relationship
between the size of the nucleus and the size of the cell.

Exceptions to these principles are found in exceptional cells:
for example, the eggs of birds and reptiles, which are of course
single cells with their accessories, may be many thousands of times
as big as the general run of cells. A very large proportion of the
matter of these cells is reserve food for the embryo that will develop; this means that the biologically active material they contain is very much less than their actual bulks and that their
surfaces are very much extended by this inflation with inactive
material. Most plant cells are also somewhat above the average

in size; they have their surfaces disproportionately increased by enormous amounts of cell sap, which distend the protoplasm.

A final word concerning the symmetry of cells, before we pass on to the structure of higher plants and animals. Primitive freely floating cells usually have a radial symmetry in all three dimensions; cut them in half in any direction and two similar halves result. Where the cells form part of an outer or an inner surface of a plant or an animal or an organ, a flattening results, restricting this radial symmetry to two dimensions only. The cell now has an inner side and an outer side or, if flattened under the influence of gravity, a top and a bottom. Another specialization, usually associated in some way with movement—of the cell, or its extremities—or with a requirement for tensile strength, results in a lengthening of the cell, giving it a spindle shape. This is again radial symmetry in two dimensions only; but the third axis is increased instead of being decreased. Finally, usually by a combination of these two stresses acting at right angles to each other, cells may be reduced to a bilateral symmetry; their fronts and backs differ, their tops and bottoms differ, but the two sides are similar. Most of this applies, too, to single-celled organisms—to protozoa and to protophyta, the simpler living things.

Out of these bricks and the various shapes into which they may be differentiated, the fascinating variety of form, of curve and symmetry and pattern, of our familiar plants and animals are derived. Out of this compromise between the biological needs of the cells and tissues and the physical or chemical dictates of their various environments and activities, come the streamlined form of a porpoise, the aerodynamic wing of a gull, the load-bearing solidity of an elephant's foot, the symmetry of spruce, the pattern of a pansy.

Colour is usually included within the scope of the study of structure; this is appropriate since many animal colours are not pigments but result from recurring minute structures the size of the wavelength of light. These are not cellular structures but inert materials laid down by cells. They break up the light into its component colours and give us the iridescence and the metallic sheen of fish and many birds and insects. Much of the most impressive pattern and symmetry of nature is like this, made of non-living materials moulded by living cells. The curvaceous shells of snails, the honeycomb of the bee, the horn of a mountain sheep, hairs, scales, and feathers, the outer body covering of insects and crustaceans, and even the wood of trees, are but the products of living things.

As with the cell, so with higher animals, size is limited principally by the relationships between surface area and volume. The biggest insects are no bigger than they are because, at least until they have finished growing, they obtain their oxygen by diffusion at a rate which depends on their surface area: but they need it at a rate which depends on their volume. And also because the support they can get from the air when flying depends on their surface area, but the weight they have to support on their volume.

A bone is strong in proportion to the area of its cross section; the pull which a muscle can exert is similarly limited. But the weight of a vertebrate animal, which the one has to support and the other has to move around, depends on its volume. Thus an elephant needs so much more bone and muscle proportionately than a mouse that it only just has room to spare for its other essential organs; and a whale cannot support itself on land and is only mobile by virtue of the buoyancy of sea water.

The symmetry of higher organisms is governed by similar prin-

Figure 16.   **A whale cannot support itself on land.**

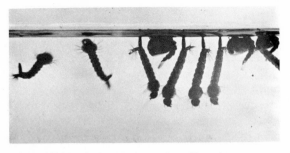

Figure 17.   A special interest in the surface film of water . . . mosquito larvae and pupae.

ciples to those governing the form of cells, except that being larger, they are more often supported, at some stage of their lives or their ancestry, on some horizontal surface, on the land or on the bottom or surface of sea or lake. If, like the plants and many animals—starfish, sea anemones, sponges—, they are anchored to this surface or move around but little, they are usually radially symmetrical in this horizontal plane, a departure from full three-dimensional symmetry forced on them by gravity, giving them a top and bottom, a dorsal and a ventral surface.

When the requirements of movement are added to this effect of gravity, we have the more familiar bilateral symmetry of most of our common animals—birds, fishes, and mammals. This means they have differing anterior and posterior ends, or fronts and backs, differing dorsal and ventral surfaces, or tops and bottoms, but similar left and right sides.

There are, of course, exceptional members of the bilateral groups of animals who, like man, have taken to going around with an abnormal orientation, with the anterior up, the posterior down, the dorsal behind and the ventral in front. And others, like back-swimming bugs and some crustacea, go about fully upside down. Examination of the structure of the internal systems of the two largest groups of these bilateral animals shows many of these to be the opposite way round. The nerve cord is dorsal in the vertebrates and ventral in the insects; the heart is dorsal in the insects and ventral in the vertebrates. One group seems somehow to have got turned upside down, perhaps on its evolutionary way from water to land; many animals in each environment take a special interest in the surface film of water and turn to face this.

It may be salutary for us to remember that we are not only on end, but may also have an upside down history. In this situation, the definitions of dorsal and ventral are open to question.

And finally there are some groups of animals, notably amongst the molluscs, in which many structures are completely asymmetrical. Very frequently amongst these, spiral or helical structures are to be found, a simple result of differing growth rates. This, as we have seen in DNA in the genes, is a convenient way of packing a lot of length into a very little space. In one group of snails a part of the nervous system is twisted, along with the part of the body containing it, into a figure-of-eight loop; and comparative studies of related species show various stages of this strange happening. If you ever stop to look, you will find that most kinds of snails usually have a right-handed twist; but in most kinds also, there are a few non-conformists who twist the other way. This has proved to be an interesting problem in genetics. Another group of molluscs, the ammonite ancestors of squid and octopus, have, in their evolution through geological time, progressively wound themselves up into a tighter and tighter spiral, only to unwind again to a form resembling that from which they started. The arrangements of leaves, branches, and floral organs in many plants also show a helical pattern which has undergone interesting evolutionary changes. Perhaps the passing fascination of 'The Twist' lies in some atavistic affinity to a similar tendency in our ancestry.

Figure 18.   **Left-handed (on the left) and right-handed snail shells.**

The overriding influence in determining the shape of higher plants and animals is the mechanical support system, the skeleton. The roots and stems of plants have the conducting transpiration system built into them and the metabolic, storage, and reproductive system hung on to them, in an arrangement appropriate to

Figure 19.   Many plants show a helical pattern.

their respective functions but dictated in detail by the environment, both dead and living. The mobility of most higher animals requires that the skeleton be strung with muscles, but in other respects their forms are dictated by considerations similar to those which apply to plants.

Anatomy really begins to hang together and give meaningful results when it is studied comparatively. Particularly when the structure of fossil forms—which are usually all that is left of extinct organisms—is brought in, comparative anatomy gives all the clues that are needed for the evolutionary concept of living things. Time and again in the history of biology, men have obtained an inkling of evolution from very limited comparative studies of the structure of animals—principally the bony structure of vertebrates —only to be, time and again, side-tracked into meaningless speculation.

Aristotle's approach was only in the smallest degree comparative; yet it appears to have been this that stimulated the clearly evolutionary viewpoint of Lucretius, eloquently expressed in these fragments of Winspear's translation of his *De Rerum Natura*:

> So earth, new-born raised herbs and shrubbery first,
> And then produced the tribes of living things—
> Those various tribes that came to be
> So variously in many ways.

and again:

> The fierce and savage race of lions through valour has survived;
> Foxes through cunning and the deer through speed.

A first objective of comparative studies is to decide which parts in one species are equivalent to which in another. This is done on the basis of their connections and can often be confirmed by studies of development in the embryo. Such equivalent parts are said to be homologous. The Frenchman Belon published a beautiful comparative study of the skeleton of man and bird, in which, as early as 1555, he correctly homologized most of the bones, but, in a most disappointing denouement concluded only that 'the structural conformity of birds with man is one of the subtleties of nature'.

With less excuse, because they had substantially more comparative studies and important homologies to guide them, at the end of the eighteenth century Goethe and his school in Germany, and Geoffroy in France, produced only a faint shadow of an evolutionary idea before becoming obsessed with a search for an unreal and speculative unity of structure. In pursuit of this, and of homologies to support it, much violence was done to the true structure of many animals.

Instead, then, of comparative anatomy providing the major insight to evolution, it took second place to natural history although Darwin says in the *Origin of Species* that it is '. . . one of the most interesting departments of natural history, and may almost be said to be its very soul'. Comparative anatomy did come into its own in support of Darwin's theories and had its heyday in the latter part of the nineteenth century.

Today, comparative anatomy usually means comparison between species, but Francis Bacon used the term with reference to

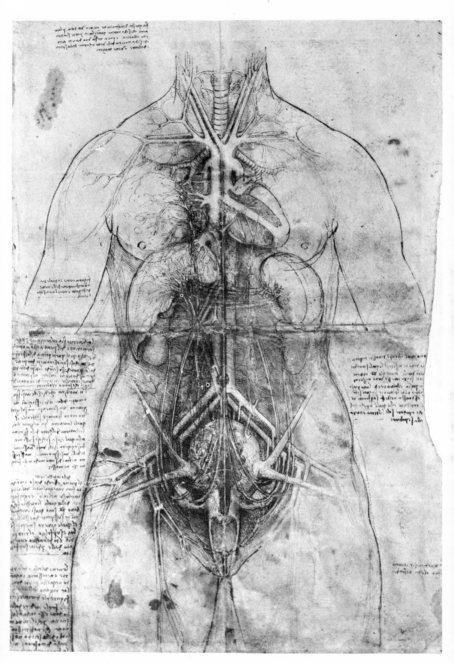

Figure 20.   A drawing by Leonardo da Vinci . . . the greatest combined artist-anatomist of all time.

comparison within species. The variation of structure within a species is usually much less than between species, and its study calls for precise measurements and statistical procedures. This, as we shall see, has become of great importance in the study of classification, a study that is still largely based on structure.

I would like now to go back to the relationship between anatomy and art, and to Leonardo da Vinci as the greatest combined artist-anatomist of all time. Few people realize the tremendous role played by animals and plants in art. Quite apart from recognized natural forms, the basilisca and the fleur-de-lis and many other almost geometrical pattern devices were derived from formalized plant and animal structures. I would like to suggest that this is perhaps itself a manifestation of structure; that forms and structures evolved from the same ancestral stock as ourselves, no matter how far back, are those most likely to evoke pleasurable sensations within our human form through our human eyes. 'Success' has been most readily achieved in the visual arts with a naturalistic approach, but this does not invalidate abstract and impressionist approaches; indeed it may explain them. Perhaps these succeed only to the extent to which they evoke, somewhere along their passage to the brain of the viewer, physiological changes that parallel, or contrast with, those evoked by natural forms.

For the biologist, accused, as he often is, of impiety in his scientific approach to the beauties of nature, in the dissection of animals and in experimenting with flowers, Leonardo is the perfect defence. This accusation is as unjust as it is ignorant. As T. H. Huxley said:

> To a person uninstructed in natural history, his country or sea-side stroll is a walk through a gallery filled with wonderful works of art, nine-tenths of which have their faces turned to the wall. Teach him something of natural history and you place in his hands a catalogue of those which are worth turning round.

Your art critic may dissect a picture with impunity. A feeling for beauty is not the prerogative of the artist and there is no essential antagonism between the arts and the sciences. The beauty of living things is more than skin deep. Those who can appreciate only the ragged dazzle of an aster or the glint of gold on a beetle's wing miss a lot. These things take on an added depth of meaning when they imply, as they do to the scientist, homologies in kinship without and cellular patterns within.

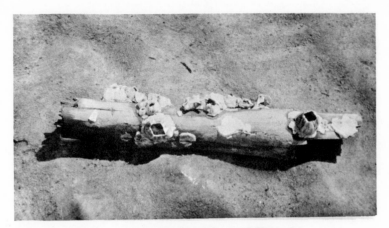

Figure 21. Suffer a sea-change; barnacles on driftwood.

4

SUFFER
A
SEA-CHANGE

genetics
and evolution

> But doth suffer a sea-change
> Into something rich and strange.
> SHAKESPEARE, *The Tempest*, I. ii

A biologist in the middle of a continent is like a fish out of water, for the seas and their shores are, biologically speaking, the most interesting places in the world. One of the more certain things about the original development of living things is that this happened in the sea. Not only this but most, if not all of the major groups of animals had their beginnings in the sea. The sea then has been most productive of organic change, at least in the animal kingdom. Perhaps the fact that man is a terrestrial animal who experiences some difficulty in observing what goes on in the sea explains his tardiness in learning about evolution.

We have seen that an evolutionary view of living things was held by Lucretius before the birth of Christ; but the recognition of evolutionary relationships goes back a lot further than this. Evolution has in fact only been forgotten through the Dark Ages and since. There are unfortunately many people alive today who are still living in the Dark Ages. They find, in general, two obstacles to emerging from this dim past: firstly, the apparent contradiction between biblical statements on the creation and the implications of evolutionary theory on this point; secondly, as a specific example of this, the idea that they themselves are descended from apes is a bitter pill to swallow.

Primitive peoples have no such problems. Their traditional knowledge from the past is less specific than the Bible (1). They recognize their affinity with the great apes of today. The natives of Borneo and Sumatra gave their great ape the name orang-utan. 'Orang' is the Malay word for 'man' and 'utan' means 'wild, of the woods': thus we have the 'wild man of the woods'. Natives of Central Africa have a similar attitude towards chimpanzees and gorillas; they live close to nature, their lives interwoven with those of many animals, and they correctly recognize their kinship with these and their particular kinship with the apes.

In his first conceit of civilization, man lost sight of his origins and foreswore his former associates of the animal kingdom. For perhaps 4,000 years he tried to go it alone, a mixed-up individual, uncertain of his origins, in quest for the meaning of his life. This meaning is evolution. Darwin's discovery—or rather rediscovery —of evolution, and also of the principal mechanism of this almost at one step, must surely rank for many millennia as one of the most important events in human history.

In our account of the origins of life we went as far as the evolution of the first cell. We saw that genes and chromosomes can duplicate themselves within the cell. This is the prelude to cell division, and cell division seems to have been the most primitive form of reproduction. It is also, of course, the way in which a plant or an animal grows from a fertilized egg. The genes carry the information that determines what the egg will grow into. Every cell in the body carries in its same genes the same information. Yet some develop into muscle cells, some into nerve cells, some into blood, bone, or sinew; while some develop into germ cells, eggs, or sperm, for the next generation. It is the environment, the internal environment in the body, that determines what a cell will become. Cells are influenced by their neighbours, and by their position and orientation. The variation between cells is thus brought about by their genetical make-up, which decides whether they will be man-cells or dog-cells or oak-tree-cells, and by their environment, which decides whether they will form parts of bone, or leaf, or brain, or root hair.

Figure 22.   Genes determine which of the snail's cells will develop into shell.

Variation is the basis of change. When you recognize your friends or relations, it is because they are different from you and from each other. In a similar way, you can recognize your own cat and distinguish it from your neighbour's, and can recognize individuals among farm animals. With less certainty, perhaps, you may be able to distinguish individual plants or individual insects, organisms less closely related to you. Even where you fail to do this, differences exist, differences that the animals themselves can recognize.

These differences between individuals are of two kinds: inborn and imprinted; the results of nature and of nurture, of parentage and of upbringing, of genetics and of environment. The relative magnitude and importance of each of these differences can be roughly assessed by considering the appearance and qualities of any identical twins you may know. In these people there are no inborn or genetical differences, only the imprinted or environmental differences remain; these, as is well known, increase with age as the environments diverge. The differences between the twins are the result of small differences of environment; the differences between them and other young people from a similar environment are genetical. Widely differing environments can, of course, produce more pronounced variation than we normally find between identical twins.

Most of the qualities that vary within a species occur most frequently at a level near to the average. People are most frequently of nearly average height, dogs of average intelligence, cabbages of average weight. The extreme individuals, tall and short people, smart and stupid dogs, light and heavy cabbages, are less common than the average individuals; the more extreme they are the less common they are. This pattern of variation is such a strikingly uniform feature of nearly all qualities of sexually reproduced organisms that the curve expressing it (obtained, for example, by plotting the numbers of individuals of each height against the height) is known as the normal frequency distribution curve; or more shortly, the normal curve. It is of great importance in understanding the mechanism of evolution by natural selection, the Darwinian explanation of how evolution occurs.

The geometrical shape of the normal curve is that of a conventional bell as seen in side view, or that obtained by drawing two S-shaped or sigmoid curves, the second backwards, united at the top. It has a hump in the middle representing the many average individuals and it tapers off gradually to the few extremes on either side.

Man has known for thousands of years that by selecting individuals at one end of this normal curve and breeding from them, he could move the average towards this end. By selecting the fattest pigs and breeding from them, he could get pigs of greater average fatness (2). He has used this principle in moulding domestic animals to his needs. It is surprising that man took so long to realize that nature could do the same thing. Yet this is the basic process of evolution. The environment, itself changing through the aeons, does the selecting, eliminating from one end of a curve of variation those individuals least fit to cope with the change, allowing those from the other end of the curve to mature and reproduce themselves. This is the simplest picture we can give, representing the way in which one quality of an organism changes in successive generations under the influence of natural selection. All the qualities of all organisms, however, are subjected to these selection pressures and one cannot of course isolate the effects on any one quality; there are interactions. The environment that is doing the selecting includes other plants and animals, in various relationships with the one under study, which are themselves being acted upon by similar selective influences.

Charles Darwin's early thinking on this question of evolution was much influenced by the famous essay of Malthus on population. It was the fact that most organisms produce so many more offspring than are required to maintain a steady population that impressed him. Natural selection depends on this; on the existence of a superabundance of variable individuals from which parents of the next generation may be selected. Some of Darwin's ideas come from still further back; from his grandfather Erasmus Darwin. Erasmus Darwin wrote many of his scientific ideas in verse—a charming habit that seems odd to us today. One cannot talk of this chapter in the discoveries of evolution without mentioning Thomas Henry Huxley, Darwin's bulldog, who, already a distinguished zoologist, was one of the first to grasp the full significance of Darwin's work and one of the most fearless in championing it in the face of religious and personal prejudice.

The *Origin of Species,* or to give its full title: *On the Origin of Species by Means of Natural Selection, or the Preservation of Favoured races in the Struggle for Life,* was published in 1859. Darwin's pocket-book for 1837 contains the words: "In June opened first notebook on transmutation of species. Have been greatly struck from about the month of previous March on the character of South American fossils and species on the Galapagos archipelago. These facts, especially latter, origin of all my views." So the book took twenty-two years to evolve as far as the first edition; it was another 13 years to the sixth edition in 1872. In 1844 Darwin wrote to Sir Joseph Hooker ". . . I am almost convinced, quite contrary to the opinion I started with, that species are not (it is like confessing a murder) immutable"; and in 1876 in his autobiography: "But then arises the doubt, can the mind of man, which has, as I fully believe, been developed from a mind as low as that possessed by the lowest animal, be trusted when it draws such grand conclusions?"

While all this was going on, Gregor Mendel, in a monastery garden near Vienna, was quietly crossing varieties of peas. The results of his work, though published, remained largely unknown until the turn of the century—a perennial warning to every scientist to study the literature before he embarks on research. Mendel, let us face it, was lucky. He happened to hit on characteristics in peas that did not vary according to the normal curve but in a simple manner between two alternatives. Plants were either tall or short, seeds smooth or wrinkled, qualities that were controlled by single genes. But there is an element of luck in most scientific discovery, and perhaps greatness lies in an ability to recognize and exploit this luck when it comes along. Thus was the science of genetics conceived; it cannot be said to have been born until 1901 when three biologists, independently, finally got around to reading Mendel's papers. Despite its forty-five years of gestation, genetics has proved a lusty youngster!

The most universal character behaving in the manner of Mendel's peas is sex. Mendel himself suggested that this might be so (3). We know now that in most bisexual organisms, sex is determined at the time of fertilization of the egg in a most chancy manner—an exact parallel, in fact, of the toss of a coin. Two chromosomes, the sex chromosomes, are responsible. All other chromosomes occur, in the normal body cells, in similar pairs. The sex chromosomes in one sex, usually the male, differ—much as the two sexes differ—and are called X- and Y-chromosomes. The other sex has a pair of X-chromosomes. In the normal division of body cells the chromosomes are duplicated and one of each pair goes to each daughter cell. But in the two peculiar divisions that give rise to the egg and sperm, there is only one duplication of the chromosomes, so that the germ cells get only one member of each pair. This is called reduction division. The number of chromosomes is reduced to half. Spermatozoa, then, are of two types: those that get an X-chromosome from this division, and those that get a Y-chromosome; but all eggs are alike in that they all get an X-chromosome. A human egg fertilized by a spermatozoon with a Y-chromosome will thereby have an X- and a Y-chromosome and will develop into a man. To produce a woman, an egg must receive its second X-chromosome from the spermatozoon. We can look on the second X-chromosome, then, as a diminutive Adam's rib.

I have spent some time on this because the efficiency of the processes of evolution is largely dependent on sexual reproduction. This peculiar reduction division, which gives rise to the germ cells, divides all the genetic material in two in each sex so that fertilization permits a different recombination of this material. The genetic composition of the offspring thus varies; this is the origin of most variation. Sexual reproduction ensures the provision of an adequate range of raw material, inborn variations, for natural selection to work on. It was a great day for evolution when this process was evolved. Few species without it have survived.

We can easily assess quantitatively the advantage conferred by sexual reproduction. Suppose, in a plant reproducing vegetatively, that is without the sexual process, four different mutations—changes in the genes themselves—occur, this will yield five genetically different types of offspring, the original form and the four changelings. If now these plants reproduce sexually, both the male and female germ cells produced could carry either the mutant or the normal gene of any of these types, so that the offspring of each type could be of any one of three kinds; they could contain two normal genes, two mutant genes, or one of each. But these could be combined in any manner with each of the three possibilities in respect of each of the other three mutant types, giving a total of 3^4 combinations or eighty-one possibilities. It is clearly much more likely that one out of eighty-one will prove favourable than that that one out of five will. In general, species that reproduce sexually, then, have a tremendous advantage in adaptability. This advantage in adaptability, however, is paid for in reduced rate of increase. Sex is usually regarded as subserving reproduction and increase in numbers; in point of fact, because it takes two individuals to produce one instead of one to produce two, because fertilization is a fusion process, sex is antagonistic to reproduction. For the sheer production of numbers, both simple division and budding are more efficient.

The essential feature of sexual reproduction is the union of two cells, usually one from each parent, gene by gene and chromosome by chromosome. With single-celled organisms, these cells may be the parents themselves; usually they are the germ cells set aside early in development. As a necessary corollary to this there must be the peculiar type of cell division we have referred to, known as reduction division, once in each cycle, otherwise each successive generation would have twice as many chromosomes as the one before it. After reduction division, each cell contains a single set of chromosomes and is said to be haploid. After fertilization each contains a double set, a condition known as diploid. Organisms may actively feed and grow at either stage. Animals usually do this while diploid, after fertilization; primitive plants often while haploid. Nearly all plants in the haploid stage in the life cycle, after reduction division and before fertilization, grow to some extent. This is perhaps a more fundamental distinction between plants and animals than the familiar one we have used so far, the presence or absence of green, photosynthetic pigment. Plants grow when haploid, animals only when diploid.

It has been suggested that the fertilization feature of sexual reproduction was an outcome of cannibalism (3). Single-celled animals engulf their food whole; they often eat their own kind, especially when crowded. It may be difficult to tell whether one individual is eating another or conjugating with it; if the nuclei fuse, there is no difference. Fertilization and cannibalism thus have much in common. But to complete the sexual cycle, before there is another cannibalistic fertilization, a reduction division to halve the chromosome number is necessary. How this first came about we know not, but it was one of the most important events in evolution. It is now known that at least in bacteria genetic recombination can occur without the sexual process, through the intervention of viruses, in a procedure not far removed from cannibalism. When a bacterium is destroyed by viruses, part of its genetic material may hitch hike on a virus particle to another bacterium, where its influence is unimpaired. This kind of fertilization by proxy is known as transduction, an important development to the bacteria, doubtless, and its discovery a contribution to our understanding of them.

That plants and animals have evolved—have changed from the

original development of living things—has not been questioned by anybody familiar with them, for perhaps fifty years, and the majority of thinking biologists accepted this on a first reading of Darwin a hundred years ago. T. H. Huxley is reported to have commented 'Why didn't I think of this?'. Although rigid proof is impossible, the evidence in support of evolution, from fossils, from comparative anatomy, from embryology (which often reflects evolutionary history), and above all from changes in plants and animals that can be seen taking place today, all points the same way. If theories are to be judged by the results they yield, there can be no question about evolution. Science knows no alternative; sentiment can support none.

On the rather different question of the mechanism of evolution, of how evolution happens, there is a little more room for argument. Here, however, there is really only one alternative to Darwinian theory, that attributed to Lamarck, which involves the inheritance of acquired characteristics. Lamarck's most important publication, *Philosophie Zoologique*, appeared in 1809, fifty years before Darwin's *Origin of Species*. In it, although belief in the inheritance of characteristics acquired through use or disuse is to be found, it takes but a minor place. The emphasis is on an idea that goes back a lot further still, the ladder of life. This idea attempts to place all organisms in a single continuous sequence like the rungs of a ladder. Apart from the fact that this does embody the principle of evolution, it bears almost no other resemblance to reality.

Many people forget that Darwin accepted the idea of the effect of use and disuse on inheritance; his four processes responsible for evolution, in order of importance, were: natural selection, the inheritance of characters acquired by use and disuse, the inheritance of direct effects of the environment, and the inheritance of variations that arise spontaneously (5).

At the beginning of this century, Darwin's last process was formally added to evolutionary theories under the name of mutationism, as a result of the work of de Vries and others. Initial enthusiasms led to its overemphasis at the expense of the remaining processes. Since then, argument has raged back and forth readjusting the balance of emphasis between these four processes. The neo-Darwinians emphasized natural selection and mutations, the so-called neo-Lamarckians, the inheritance of acquired characteristics. But it is becoming extremely difficult to find a biologist to support this concept today. It is impossible to prove that this never happens; but a very large amount of research has been carried out on this question, with negligible evidence in favour of it. Superficially and on first acquaintance, this theory of use and disuse seems attractive and reasonable. It is comforting to believe that if one works hard, the resulting improvement in one's bodily or mental abilities will be passed on to posterity; at least it is comforting to the industrious before they reproduce. This seems to be the attraction of neo-Lamarckian theories to the Lysenkoist school in Russia. But the dwindling in evolution of an unused part and the development of a used one can be equally well explained by natural selection. A part that is of use to an animal has survival value, and individuals with the part well developed will mature and reproduce at the expense of those with it less well developed. If a part is of no use to an animal its absence or reduced size has survival value too, and individuals without it will reproduce selectively. Such is the pressure of the environment that organisms cannot afford to carry useless structures.

Lamarckian evolution demands that every part of the organism must contribute towards the offspring; that the germ cells, sperm and ovum, must therefore carry something from every part of the body. This idea is sometimes called pangenesis. But as Aristotle pointed out, if a man and woman, either of whom has lost an arm or a leg, have a baby, the baby is not on this account born without it. The germ cells do, of course, carry something *to* every part of the body; they determine the details of structure, and if the structure functions well in the environment their cellular offspring survive into the next generation. Evolution may be said to keep structure and function in step.

We should mention briefly one other type of evolutionary theory, orthogenesis. The supposition here is that evolution has a directional purposiveness; that a principle within an organism controls the direction of its subsequent changes. These theories, in their various forms, are not susceptible to experimental verification, nor necessarily incompatible with other theories. They can be neither proved nor disproved.

The most respected current opinion supports the neo-Darwinian

Figure 23. The horse . . . modern outcome of one evolutionary sequence . . . sketched by Leonardo da Vinci.

concept of natural selection acting on variations initially produced by mutation in the genes but exploited by genetic recombination. This is the way in which those who have studied it most closely believe that evolution occurs.

Fossils have played a very important role in establishing the belief that animals have changed and diversified from a limited number of original simple organisms, and some knowledge of fossils is necessary to an understanding of evolution. Men have tried to explain these fascinating relics in other ways. The bodies of sinners drowned in the Flood? But most of our fossils are of known marine or at least aquatic forms. Such catastrophic destruction could only have resulted in a gradual reduction in the number of species. All our evidence points the other way. Perhaps twelve million different kinds of plants and animals exist today; for earlier epochs the number known is progressively smaller the further back we go; this is not only due to lack of knowledge.

Working forwards in time from the oldest fossil-bearing strata, in many groups of plants and animals gradual progressive changes can be traced, some of them continuously up to familiar present-day species. Other groups disappear suddenly from the record, never to reappear. Even if we have no clear records of the natural formation of new species since science began, we have plenty of records, all too intimate, of their extinction. This was at one time denied in theological doctrine; even the doctrine of special creation evolves!

It is strange that North America, where the economy has depended so largely on the practical developments from the theory of evolution, on the use of index fossils in prospecting for oil and gas and other minerals, should be such a stronghold of medievalism on this question. Were creationists to think about this, they would surely return to the horse and buggy for transportation; for there would be little oil to be had without a knowledge of evolution. They would then have constantly before them as they travelled, today's outcome of one of the best-documented evolutionary sequences.

5

A PLACE
FOR
EVERYTHING

systematics
and classification

A place for everything,
and everything in its place.
SMILES, *Thrift*, ch. 5

In classifying plants and animals, we use both what we know of their structure and what this tells us of their evolution. I would like first to describe how this is done and how scientific names are given, and then to outline the results of this, the classification of plants and animals in use today.

The immediate practical concern of much work on the classification of plants and animals is to provide a convenient, tidy system into which present-day species can be pigeon-holed, from which they can be recovered, and with the aid of which they can be identified: a place for everything and everything in its place. Studies on an organism can hardly be begun until it has a name and a recognizable description attached to it. This was the outlook of the early workers in this field of biology. Karl Linnaeus, the eighteenth-century Swedish father of classification, collected and classified and described not only plants and animals but also almost anything that could be subjected to this treatment.

But the true purpose, the ultimate and unattainable objective of systematic studies is to draw the entire family tree of all the organisms that have ever lived: to unravel the relationships of this species to that species, this family to that family, today, yesterday, and back to the origins of life. As if this were not enough, systematics concerns itself too with variation within a species, with sub-species and varieties and with the processes by which they become species. When all of this is done, it will only be necessary to keep up with evolutionary changes as they occur, and indulge in pleasant speculation regarding the future. But by contrast with the tidy practical system, our knowledge here is as yet so scanty and scrappy that modern classification is a most untidy affair.

While it is true that systematic work is at the base of biology, it is also, in its modern outlook, at the apex. No organism can be assuredly placed in its family tree without taking into consideration every scrap of information about it—its structure, function, biology, development, and so on. The systematist provides a handle for workers in other fields to use; he expects in return, data from these other workers which he can use to improve the handle, or its orientation. We may regard classification as a sort of bank of biological knowledge.

I have used the term species, which I have so far defined as the entire population of a particular kind of plant or animal. This begs the question, substituting the word 'kind' for the word 'species'. We must now define a species more rigidly, but this is the only grouping in classification for which this can be done. A species is usually defined as a group of populations that can or could interbreed between and within themselves but that cannot interbreed with other such groups. This is a good practical definition for present-day living populations and can be applied quite well to some groups of recent fossils. Where a whole group has become extinct, it is necessary to make a judgement on the basis of experience with living groups. The differences between species in these living groups are a guide to what may be expected in related fossils.

A species originates by the separation of two populations of a pre-existing species: either physical separation by an upthrust of mountains or an inflow of water, or perhaps separation by behaviour and habits. Natural selection acts differently on the two populations. Each is changed by selection to suit its own environment, and other changes linked to these gradually, through many generations, reduce the extent to which the two groups can interbreed until they may be said to be 'good and distinct species'. The process is usually very gradual and it is impossible to draw a line and say 'here we have one species, and here we have two'. Occasionally one or more profound mutations, sudden changes in the genes, or perhaps wholesale changes in the chromosomes oc-

54

cur and the line is then clear cut. There is a fork in the family tree. It is rare to find convincing evidence in fossils for these sudden changes of species, and it is now generally held that the great majority of these changes are in fact of a gradual character. The origin of species, then, is usually gradual, tapered, and vague; but partly indeed because these changes are so slow, the difference in form between two species at any given time is usually quite clear.

So much for the origin of a species. Its end comes about in one of two ways: either it fails to adapt fast enough, closely pursued by a changing environment, and becomes extinct, or it breaks up into two more forms, both of which are so different that it seems unlikely that either could have bred with the original. It is usually impossible to say for sure whether any generation of a species could have bred with any preceding generation, although an experienced biologist can usually express an opinion based on the nature and extent of differences in the structure of related present-day species that live together. In these difficult cases, we may truly say that a species is what a good systematist says it is.

The systematists then are in a dilemma. Their task is to describe and name and classify, in a system of distinct units, populations of plants and animals that are not really distinct but that, if traced back far enough in time, grade into each other. At the same time this is a most necessary practical requirement; nearly all biological workers depend on systematists to name the species they work with.

Now that we know what a species is, let us consider the names of some in more detail. The system of naming in universal use today is that introduced by John Ray in England and firmly established by Linnaeus. This is a system similar to Christian names and surnames except that it is the other, the sensible, way round, with the larger grouping first. It is known as the binomial system. In Linnaeus's time, Latin was the most widely understood language, so two Latin names are used, one for the genus, which is a group of species, and one for the species. These names are understood by biologists of all countries, although the same can no longer be said of Latin. Generic names are very frequently the Latin or Greek names for the plants or animals in the genus; and since many of our common names come from Latin or Greek, these are usually easy to understand: *Populus* for poplar, *Pinus* for pine, *Falco* for falcon, *Ursus* for bear. Specific names are usually adjectives qualifying the noun of the genus: *Populus tremuloides*, the trembling poplar or aspen, *Pinus contorta*, the twisted or lodgepole pine, *Falco peregrinus*, the wandering or peregrine falcon, *Ursus horribilis*, the horrible or grizzly bear.

Linnaeus arranged the species in both the plant and the animal kingdoms in hierarchies of groupings to which he gave the names, class, order, and genus. Although we have seen that only the species can be defined, we have described a genus as a group of species. These species have a common origin more or less distinct from other such groups. Many a genus and species described by Linnaeus in his *Systema Naturae* in 1758, especially in the plants, stands almost unchanged today, although the genus has mostly become a somewhat smaller group. His larger groupings, however, orders and classes, have proved quite inadequate and others have had to be interpolated. These groupings are the phylum, between kingdom and class, and the family, not to be confused with the conventional use of this word, a half-way grouping between order and genus. A family in the everyday sense with its family name or surname is a group consisting of one male and one female and their offspring. In the systematic sense, a family may include scores of genera, hundreds of species, within each of which there may be millions of families in the everyday sense. In many places it is also necessary to fill in with sub- and super-groups between most of the main groupings. We thus have, in ascending order, sub-species, species, and super-species, sub-genus, genus, and on through family, order, and class to phylum, super-phylum, sub-kingdom, and kingdom (1).

We might perhaps take one example to show the way in which this system operates. Let us take one close to home. The name Linnaeus used for the human species was *Homo sapiens*. Because he described it in the tenth edition of his *Systema Naturae* in 1758, which has been set as a sort of a deadline in nomenclature, his name, or more often just the initial letter L is placed after it lest anybody else should, unaware of Linnaeus's description, describe some other species, perhaps the abominable snowman, and give it the same name. Man, then, is *Homo sapiens* L. or *Homo sapiens* Linnaeus. The two names again are Latin, the first, *homo*, meaning 'man', is the name of the genus, the second, *sapiens*, meaning 'the reasoner', the name of the species. Linnaeus described only one other species in the same genus as man, namely *Homo troglodytes* L., man the cave dweller; this was Linnaeus's name for the orang-utan, rather far removed from the cave man and now placed in a different genus in a different family. We now have several other species included in the genus *Homo*, but all of them are fossil, such as *Homo neanderthalensis*, Neanderthal man. But *Homo* is not the only genus of men; there are other fossil species such as those in the genus *Pithecanthropus*, Java man and Pekin man. All are included with the genus *Homo* in the same family, the Hominidae. Our friend the orang-utan is now placed in the family Pongidae. Both families are in the order Primates, which includes all the monkeys, in the class Mammalia, the mammals, in the phylum Chordata—having backbones or something similar.

Much confusion is caused, and indeed much harm is done to the science of systematics by the duplication of names, especially those of species. This confusion is caused by the failure of some workers to assimilate all previous work and knowledge on the group of their choice, before adding to this in print. The accepted and necessary law of priority states roughly that the first published name for a species is correct—back in 1758, the tenth edition of Linnaeus's *Systema Naturae* (2). If a worker in ignorance of the existence of an earlier name proposes another one for the same species, this will eventually become a synonym, a name attached to nothingness, an empty shell of knowledge. The scientific literature in biology contains thousands such, a permanent record of superficiality among its workers. This is a field in which the materials of research are specimens and books. Workers in it must have both abundantly.

Let us turn now to the other end of the scale, to the largest grouping, the phylum. This is a distinctive group of plants or animals, having a common structural plan differing from that of other such groups. Agassiz described a phylum as an idea and a class as a way of expressing that idea. Biologists have devoted much time and effort towards elucidating the relationships between the phyla. That is, to the study of phylogeny. It must be admitted that this has been rather unfruitful. Three main types of information have been used: that from fossils, that from comparative anatomy, and that from development or embryology. In some respects at least, the embryological development of an individual animal recapitulates the evolutionary development of the species, so that relationships which are obscure in the adult may be revealed by the embryo or larva. Some relationships are clearly established. The difficulty with the remainder may well be that they do not exist; that some phyla or groups of phyla are completely unrelated to others, and represent separate developments from separate origins of living matter. About twenty phyla of animals are recognized, eight phyla of plants, and a further six phyla of primitive single-celled organisms such as bacteria in the border country between plants and animals. When we get back to these single-celled organisms, the differences between plants and animals seem less striking than the differences between single-celled and many-celled forms in either kingdom. Thus many of these simple forms are grouped as a third kingdom known as the Protista. Increased recognition is being given to the importance of the cell nucleus in classification; the bacteria and the blue-green algae lack this structure and may be treated as another separate kingdom, the Monera.

About a million different species of animals, of which three-quarters are insects, and two hundred and fifty thousand species of plants have been scientifically described and named. Reliable estimates of the actual numbers of species of the insects, based on the rate at which species are being newly described and on changes in this rate over the years, indicate that many million species of these ubiquitous animals exist on this earth (3). For every species described there may be ten as yet unknown. If this applies on the average for other organisms, twelve million species of plants and animals must exist. Yet this process of describing and naming is but the first foundation step in biological science; until this step has been taken nothing else can begin. It is a sobering thought that far more money is being spent on research in other fields of biology, and especially in applied biology, than in this very basic field. Progress indeed is so slow that one may legitimately wonder whether man will succeed in classifying the bulk of his fellow organisms before they—or he—have evolved into something different.

We have seen that systematics must be largely based on structure, on comparative studies of structure between related species. Among many groups, and especially among the insects, themselves often minute, the structural differences between one species and the next may be extremely small; especially when the species are closely related. We have seen too, that there may be quite extensive variation, in form and colour, as well as other characteristics, within a species. How then are we to distinguish between the two; between variation within a species, and variation that indicates a difference between species? This is where measurements and statistical procedures are important. Wherever possible, features that can be counted are used; the number of joints in an appendage, or the number of hairs on a plate of the body; these too may vary of course, but limits can be set to the variation known to occur in a given species by counting, without recourse to measurement. But sooner or later this becomes necessary.

If then we measure, say, the left hind leg of each of a hundred specimens of what we believe to be a single species of beetle, and draw a graph of the number of specimens with legs of a given length against the magnitude of this length, we should expect to get a normal frequency distribution curve, that is a curve with a single central hump at the average length and a gradual tailing off in numbers of specimens with either very long or very short left hind legs. Should we get a curve with two peaks and a trough between them, we would suspect that we really had two different species of beetles.

Much of the variation within species is variation in size; specimens may be small as a result of malnutrition, or large as a result of good feeding. These effects can be eliminated by measuring two structures or two dimensions in each specimen and dividing one by the other. Thus, taken together, these measurements give us a ratio, which is independent of size.

The amount of variation can of course be expressed statistically for each of two species, and if there is some overlap in size or proportions this may be necessary. The probability that a particular specimen belongs to the one or the other species can then also be given mathematical expression. We may give an example of this in our own genus: if the cranial capacity of adult man, *Homo sapiens*, is measured the average value found is 1,350 cubic centimetres. The value found for the extinct Neanderthal man is 1,450 cubic centimetres. A skull with 1,400 cubic centimetres capacity is about equally likely to have belonged to a representative of either species on the basis of this character. Incidentally, the extinction of Neanderthal man should provide food for some thoughts in our—smaller—brains.

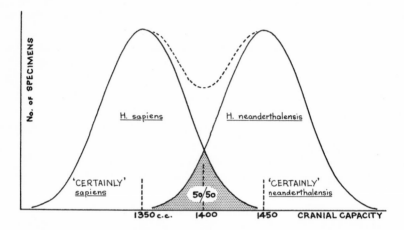

Figure 24. **Species overlap.**

One other complication is important in systematic work. A great many animals and plants pass through a number of changes of form in their lives. These may be so pronounced that the different stages of one species may be described as different species. Eggs of insects have been described both as seeds and as stages of a moss. Since classification depends on form, a good description includes accounts of all three, four, or more stages—the egg, larva, pupa, and adult, of an insect; the sexual and the more familiar stages of a fern, and so on. It may be necessary to rear the various stages in a laboratory, or even to wait perhaps as long as twenty years for them to be produced in nature. This is one thing that limits the rate at which systematic work can proceed; perhaps it is also one of its attractions in these days of deadlines. This branch of biology owes much to the patient labours of amateurs whose studies of living things 'for the love of them' are an eloquent testimony to the fascination this field can exert.

We have dealt with some of the main principles in systematic work; let us now take a quick look at the results of this, at the classifications of living plants and animals (4, 5), while not forgetting the fascinating fossils that we shall have to leave out. If we stay at the phylum level these will be few: most of the major designs of living things have survived in some form until today.

The six phyla of Protista, in the border country between plants and animals, we can acknowledge only by name: bacteria, flagellates, amoeboids, ciliates, sporozoa, and slime moulds.

Back at the beginning of the plant kingdom we have no less than five phyla of algae—pond weeds, and seaweeds, ranging from the minute and often radially symmetrical diatoms to the giant ribbon-like marine *Laminaria*, over two hundred feet long. These are the experimental plants that have been, so to speak, playing around with pigments. The phyla differ mainly in colour —reds, greens, and browns—and in details of the life cycle.

Then the fungi: the moulds, the yeasts, and the mushrooms, a rather decadent group of plants, which have given up pigments and taken to feeding mostly on the dead remains of more conventional plants. This has proved profitable; many thousand species have been described.

The mosses and liverworts, the first truly terrestrial green plants, have the peculiar feature of spending most of their lives with only a single set of chromosomes. Although terrestrial, they are only found in wet situations because the male reproductive cells, like animal sperm, are free swimming so that fertilization can only occur when the plants are wet.

The last phylum, the vascular plants, includes most of our more familiar species: club-mosses, horsetails, ferns, the coniferous trees, and the latest flowering of the plant kingdom, the vast and glorious assemblage of the flowering plants. They have learnt to lift water above ground. Reproductive cells of both sexes are usually produced on the same plant, but many devices for cross-fertilization have been developed. These, and other specializations account for the fact that two-thirds of the plant species are in this group.

Figure 25.
Liverworts.

Figure 26.
Sponges—
-Venus' flower
basket.

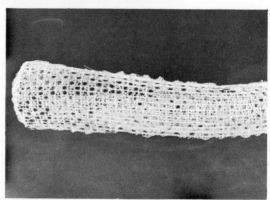

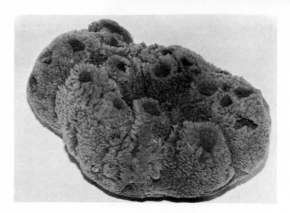

Figure 27.
Sponges—
-bath sponge.

Among the animals those most simply organized are the 4,000-odd species of sponges, in which only two layers of cells are to be found, although these may be complexly folded. Ousted from our bathtubs by plastic upstarts, they are likely to become for most people, curiosities. Also with only two layers, but the inventors of the stomach, are the jellyfish with some 10,000 species. Their stomachs communicate with the outside world by a single channel, used as both entrance and exit. A great many of the flatworms, a still larger group with some 15,000 species, live a complex parasitic life with a sequence of different forms in a sequence of hosts. The third layer of cells in the development of the body first appears in this group.

We must pass over a number of groups of worms, with many thousands of species between them, despite the obvious importance of many of them as parasites, and in the sea and in the soil. In these groups stomachs with separate entrances and exits may be found. The last of these, the segmented worms, including our familiar earthworm, leeches, and many and varied marine species, is of special interest by virtue of its segmentation, foreshadowing that of both the largest of all groups of organisms, the arthropods, and of the group in which we ourselves belong, the chordates.

The arthropods with nearly a million species are a testimony to tubular construction; they combine the functions of skin and skeleton in one rugged body covering. Because of this their joints are showing; this does not embarrass them, but the resulting necessity to moult in order to grow does. In the soft, white nakedness of their new skins, palatable, defenceless, and unable to bite back, they are often decimated by predatory relatives; this is their weakness. Most of them are insects, the only animals without backbones that can fly and the world's most marvellous animals. The sea, however, has defeated them, but another arthropod group the crustacea, shrimps, crabs, lobsters, and the like, has done nearly as well there. Spiders, mites, ticks, centipedes, millipedes, all are included in this tremendous assemblage.

Two rather isolationist phyla remain before our own, the chordates. The molluscs, some 100,000 species of them, make up an ancient and largely herbivorous group, strangely asymmetrical, ranging from primitive-seeming sluggish snails to highly specialized and active predators, full of nous, the octopuses, cuttlefish, and the giant squids that may reach a length of over fifty feet, and which lie behind many a mariner's tale of sea serpents. The other phylum, the echinoderms with their peculiar five-rayed symmetry, exclusively marine, is one of the hardest groups to understand. The starfish and sea urchins with the mouth in the middle below and the anus in the middle above, crawl rather slowly but powerfully over the sea bottom, yet prey on other active animals. Others, the sea cucumbers, go about on their sides; still others, the sea lilies, upside down. These, despite their names, are both animals.

The chordates include a few groups of small marine animals, the sea squirts and amphioxus, which seem to be trying out the ideas for the vertebrates and which reflect the echinoderms in their development, and then the great vertebrate groups themselves: the highly successful fish with some 23,000 species; the amphibious amphibia, animal mosses, leading to our familiar terrestrial groups; the reptiles, diverse and widespread relics of a success long past; the birds, light-weight warm-blooded reptiles with scales frayed into feathers; and finally, the mammals, of which you and I represent one among 4,500 species. These imposing beasts are to be found, like insects, in most habitats, but unlike them, also in the sea.

We have mentioned a vast array of plant and animal neighbours. They are worth knowing; and there is a lifetime of satisfying work for systematists in every group.

6

GREEN
FUSE

the study
of function

The force that through
the green fuse drives the flower . . .
DYLAN THOMAS, *Collected Poems
1934-1952*

The study of the functions of plants and animals, what makes
them go, live and move, and have their being, is known as physiology, and like their classification it depends on structure, on how
they are put together. I shall first describe the chemistry of the
plant and animal and how this leads to growth and reproduction
and provides the organism with energy; then how this energy is
used by the organism in responding to its environment. It is only
when we come to look at how an animal works that we begin to
understand the meaning of its structure; the long neck of a giraffe
is a rather meaningless thing until its function is known, browsing
the leaves off tallish trees, say acacias. The tallness of the acacia
in turn is also meaningless if one does not understand that the
function of the leaves demands that they be at the top to absorb
the energy of sunlight.

The structural quality of tallness in acacias has evolved because
of its functional advantages, with less shadowing by other trees
and hence more hours of sunlight, and less loss of leaves by the
browsing of animals. In both the animal and the plant, function
points the meaning to structure. There is thus a basic borderline
field between structure or anatomy and function or physiology—
usually called functional anatomy, though it could equally well be
called structural physiology.

The relationships between the tree and the giraffe and between
both of these and sunlight are not really the concern of the physi-

ologist, but come into the domain of ecology, the topic of my next chapter. The physiologist is concerned with the workings of plants and animals as individuals, with their internal workings rather than their external workings. The more sophisticated physiologists are inclined to ignore functional anatomy and often concentrate their attention on the functioning of only one organ or one organ system, often in only one kind of animal or plant or at best in a small group of these, perhaps in a comparative way. This is un-

Figure 28. **The function of a long neck.**

desirable because it may mean losing sight of the whole organism, plant or animal. It is undesirable too because in biology the whole is more than the sum of the parts; in biology two and two do not necessarily make four. One may understand kidney function and liver function, heart function and lung function, brain function and the function of the other organs and systems of the body; but this does not mean to say that one can understand the animal as a whole. In so far as we do understand the functioning of plants and animals today, we can explain these in terms of physical and chemical processes. To this extent, physiology is largely biophysics and biochemistry, or perhaps bio-physical chemistry. The tendency of physiologists to restrict themselves to single organs or organ systems may be a measure of the inadequacy of contemporary physics and chemistry to deal fully with biological problems.

The general activities of the tissues of a plant or the body of an animal as it goes about its daily business of feeding and growing fall into two groups. Firstly there are the building-up processes, nutrition, absorption, transport and storage. These processes require energy, which they obtain from the second group of activities, the breaking-down processes of transport, respiration, and disposal or excretion. Respiration, breathing and the purposes it serves, of which the external evidence is the taking in of oxygen and the passing out of carbon dioxide, is the essential and basic energy-providing process in both plants and animals. In the simplest terms it is a process of burning or oxidation in which the fuel is most frequently sugars or complexes of these, although often fats and sometimes proteins. All of these substances can, of course, be burnt in a conventional manner in a fire; when the final end products are energy as heat, and usually carbon dioxide and water. So it is in a plant or animal; the raw materials are the same, the end products are the same; but the processes are different. The oxidation proceeds through a complex series of steps involving many other chemical substances, each step controlled by its own enzyme, a biochemical catalyst, facilitating the change. Perhaps the most striking way in which the process differs from a fire is its versatility. The energy may be manifest not only as heat but also as muscular or other mechanical activity, as sound resulting from this, as light in fireflies and deep-sea fishes, even as electricity in the electric eel.

A few exceptional organisms use other chemical changes not involving oxygen to obtain energy. These are of special interest since the earliest living things must have been of this type; neither carbohydrates nor oxygen were available to them.

Since in general carbohydrate fuel is converted to carbon dioxide, which is expired, and water, which is evaporated, respiration involves loss of weight. This applies to all of the breaking-down processes, in contrast to the building-up processes. In other words, growth, of which the simplest expression is increase in weight, represents the excess of the building-up processes over the breaking-down processes. The physiologist refers to these processes collectively as metabolism; growth then is equal to the excess of anabolism, the building-up processes, over katabolism, the breaking-down processes.

In problems of respiration small size is a great advantage, mainly because the surface area of the body is so much greater in proportion to its bulk, and also because the gases, oxygen and carbon dioxide, have shorter distances to travel between even the most central tissues and the exterior. This is one respect in which insects have an advantage over vertebrates; they can get away with a very much simpler breathing system. In the matter of water balance, however, the tables are turned. This is a matter of great importance in all living things since body chemicals are transported in solution in water and since, especially in plants, structural strength and many cell activities depend on the maintenance of turgor in the cells, that is, on keeping them inflated with water. A plant short of water is like a car on flat tires. For the same reasons that carbon dioxide can more readily leave an insect's body than a vertebrate's so can water vapour. Terrestrial insects thus live in constant danger of drying up; aquatic ones, by a reverse effect, of bursting through the diffusion of water inwards. Water, as we have seen, is drawn into cells by the solutions within them, the process known as osmosis.

The problem of how a plant such as a giant redwood can raise water to a height of 350 feet above the ground from a depth of many feet below it, was for many years a challenging one. Men were familiar with the fact that the best a suction pump can manage is a lift of about 30 feet, a column of water equivalent to the pressure of the atmosphere. The continuous column of water in a tree is like a train with a locomotive at each end. Osmosis draws water in through the root hairs and pushes from the bottom; evaporation or transpiration through the stomata in the leaves and surface tension in the vascular system pull from the top. Cohesive forces couple the molecules in the fine tubes in between. The higher plants cannot, like animals, move bodily in search of water, but they have a remarkable ability, all the same, to go out and get it. A plant of rye, for example, may have a total root length of over 350 miles, and may grow over 5 miles of root and develop 100 million root hairs in a day (1).

In addition to the gas exchange of respiration, metabolism is accompanied by the formation of solid end products, some of which may be toxic. The selective removal of these products, principally rather simple nitrogenous compounds, is the process known as excretion. Whether this function is fulfilled by a contractile vacuole of an amoeba, a nephridium of a worm, a malpighian tubule of an insect, or a vertebrate kidney, these materials are removed from the body *via* the blood in solution in water, so that this is another function which is impaired when water is short. When this is so, and in small terrestrial animals generally, most of this water is reabsorbed into the body before the urine is released. Other ingredients of the blood may also be withdrawn in the urine dissolved in the excess water and then reabsorbed with this. The kidneys thus take much of the responsibility for maintaining an appropriate chemical environment inside the animal, with the cooperation of the liver which transforms the principal products into a form which the kidneys can handle. As Dinesen said: "What is man, when you come to think upon him, but a minutely set, ingenious machine for turning, with infinite artfulness, the red wine of Shiraz into urine?" A bit of an exaggeration, perhaps, in view of the rather small nitrogen content of wine.

Although the profits of metabolism are growth, growth is a great deal more than just an increase in weight. The increase must come in the right place at the right time. In the egg, our giraffe's neck was no longer than yours or mine was; it was longer at birth because it grew faster. It is the different growth rates of the various organs in different directions that account for the differences between species, both among plants and animals. The complete changes of form that many insects undergo at least once during their life cycle, from maggot to fly, from caterpillar to chrysalis to butterfly, have intrigued naturalists for centuries. The realization of the importance of these changes in relation to the general questions of growth and development has led to more intensive studies of them. It is largely from these that we have learnt what we know about the development of form. This appears to depend on local variations in the internal chemical environment under the control of genes; in much the same way as hormones, or chemical messengers, control the development of the structural differences between the sexes, under the influence of the genes in the sex chromosomes. It is somewhere along this chain of influences that the drug thalidomide makes its rather sinister presence felt in the development of the human embryo.

We have seen that nearly all animals are ultimately dependent on plants for food and that the green plants are the only organisms that are able to use the radiant energy of sunlight to build up sugars and more complex carbohydrates from water and carbon dioxide. The energy resources of all living things derive ultimately from the sun, most of them through the agency of the green plants with their pigment, chlorophyll, and their building-up or anabolic process, photosynthesis. Let us then take a closer look at this process essential to modern life. Van Helmont in the seventeenth century found that a potted willow tree gained more weight than the soil it grew in lost. Joseph Priestley more than a hundred years later found that while both a mouse and a potted plant died when enclosed in separate glass jars, they lived when they **were** both enclosed together in the same. jar. The weight gain of Van Helmont's willow came both from water from the soil and carbon dioxide from the air, built up by photosynthesis into carbohydrates. Priestley's mouse was kept alive by oxygen produced by the plant, and the plant was kept alive by carbon dioxide produced by the mouse; a pretty demonstration of the interdependence of the two kingdoms, plant and animal. Neither man understood the processes involved, which indeed are still not fully known, but their findings laid the foundations of our understanding.

What is chlorophyll, the wonderful pigment that does this? Chemically it is strangely similar to haemoglobin, the red pigment of vertebrate blood, with magnesium atoms in place of the iron. Physically it absorbs the high-energy ultra-violet, violet, and red rays of the spectrum, which is why plants are green, a blend of the remaining colours. It apparently uses this energy in the first step of the sugar-making process—the splitting of water into oxygen, which is released, and hydrogen, which starts off on a series of complex reactions with carbon dioxide to form sugar (2).

When adequate growth is attained, both in plants and animals, the chemistry of the organism begins to be redirected towards the growth of the next generation, towards reproduction. We have seen that sex is determined by the chromosomes and that its expression, like all differential growth, is under the control of hormones. When sexual development is complete, fertilization and reproduction proceed to round out the life cycle. In primitive single-celled organisms, which reproduce simply by dividing in two, death and reproduction are synonymous; or if you like, there is no death, save accidental death, only reproduction. Old amoebae never die, they only divide in two. In the more complex organisms, in which groups of cells are specialized for various purposes, only the reproductive cells or germ cells, among the first to be set aside, may have immortality; the rest pay the price of specialization, they get old and die.

This process of ageing or senescence is one of a number of which we have, as yet, but little understanding. Exhaustion, fatigue, sleep, hibernation, are obviously related to it. When an animal uses up all its food reserves it may die of exhaustion; the gas tank is empty and it stops. Fatigue resembles exhaustion, but is the result of the accumulation of the products of activity rather than the running out of raw materials. During sleep and hibernation, and a similar condition known as diapause which often intervenes in the life cycles of insects, activity is reduced and metabolism slows, sometimes to an extremely low level. This is another area in which studies of insects have borne fruit in other fields. All of these processes, exhaustion, fatigue, sleep, hibernation, and diapause, are reversible; ageing and death resemble them except in that they cannot be reversed, save only in the formation of germ cells by reduction division, truly the elixir of life.

So much for the course of life, for growth, reproduction, and death, as the physiologist sees them. You will realize that here we have simply been taking a closer look, a largely biochemical look, at one of our characteristics of living things, growth and reproduction. Another field that has had much attention from physiologists recently is a further characteristic of living things, the response to stimuli.

If one places a potted plant in a dark box into which light is admitted through a small hole in one side, the plant grows towards the hole. This is a result of a strange paradox. Although plants as we have seen depend on light for their growth, nevertheless the more brightly lit a plant is, the more slowly its length increases. To return to our plant in a dark box, the shaded side, away from the source of light elongates more rapidly than the side towards it, turning the shoot towards the light. Any deviation of growth from the direction of the light is self-correcting by this simple device. This is a direct effect of light on the production of growth-regulating hormones in the growing cells of the plant shoot. Most responses of plants are of this nature, direct, slow changes. Exceptions are to be found in some seed-dispersal mechanisms, in the traps of some insectivorous plants, and in the dramatic leaf-folding mechanisms of the sensitive plants. But in general, plant responses are rather simple direct movements, in which the motion comes from changes in fluid pressure within certain key cells. Stimuli from light, gravity, moisture, and movement, are the most important.

In primitive animals, too, responses are usually simple, slow, and frequently brought about by chemical means. But quite early on in the evolution of animals two types of specialized cells appeared. One type, nerve cells, serves for communication. These cells have long fibres, running out from a central cell body, which transmit electrical changes. The other type, muscle cells, is specialized for movement, by shortening in one direction while broadening in the others. Muscle cells make use of the energy provided by respiration for mechanical purposes such as movement of the animal as a whole, or of its parts relative to each other.

The transmission of a nerve impulse is not simply that of a flow of electricity through a wire; it is much slower than this, its speed ranges from something not much better than a snail's pace to over 200 miles an hour. The speed at which nerve impulses travel is usually so much greater in large animals that the time it takes animals to react to a stimulus is much the same whatever their size. It is easy to see how natural selection could have brought this about by eliminating the slow reacters.

But the chemical method of communication found in plants and primitive animals is not entirely replaced by nerve communication. When electrical changes reach the end of a nerve fibre what happens to them? The nerve fibre may end at a muscle directly, or the impulse may have to pass through a series of nerve fibres like a bucket brigade before reaching its destination, which may include a number of different muscles. In either case, it seems that there is no continuous arrangement for electrical transmission, but a small gap remains. It is here that chemistry comes in; both from nerve fibre to nerve fibre and from nerve fibre to muscle, the transmission is a chemical one. When electrical changes reach the end of a nerve fibre they cause the release of a substance that diffuses across the minute gap and starts off either electrical changes in the other nerve, or contraction in the muscle. This substance is another hormone. Still other hormones handle much of the general internal information of the body. Released into the blood stream from the ductless glands, they can influence quite rapidly any organ that the blood reaches. If nerves are the telephones of communication, hormones are the radio.

Nerve fibres are sensitive to all kinds of physical and chemical stimulation, providing this is vigorous enough, but in most higher animals there are at least some organs of special sensitivity—eyes, ears, noses, and so on, which are generously supplied with nerve endings. These sense organs are designed to facilitate the reception of particular kinds of stimuli, eyes to receive light, ears to receive sound. But this can only be done by making them much less sensitive to all other kinds. We can easily see that the nerve endings in the eye are still sensitive, for example, to pressure. Close your eyes and press on the eyeball with a finger at the outside corner of the socket. Spots will appear before your eyes although no light, only pressure, is being received. The brain can interpret stimuli received via the optic nerve only as light stimuli. The stars one sees as a result of a blow on the eye are pressure stars.

Many special senses are found in animals. Aquatic animals have a sense of depth or hydrostatic pressure; most of those that fly have a sense of air speed. The echo-sounding system whereby many bats can detect their prey and avoid obstacles in total darkness is, of course, an extension of hearing, but may well be regarded as a separate sense. Senses of temperature, moisture, balance, and pain, and other internal senses, are widely found (3).

Not only do different animals have different senses, but the range of sensitivity varies. The so-called silent dog-whistle produces a note beyond the range of human hearing but within that of a dog. The auditory range of many insects extends two octaves beyond the upper frequency limit of man, which itself may vary by more than an octave. This is to be expected since the devices insects use to produce sounds are so much smaller that the frequencies at which they vibrate must be higher. The sounds insects make in communicating with each other can be detected by man only with special devices. Although most of this communication is related to the bringing together of the two sexes (as indeed is much of human communication), there is evidence that, especially in social insects like ants and bees, conversations of hitherto unsuspected complexity may go on.

Most people who have anything to do with other animals are familiar with the fact that there are pronounced differences in vision even between quite closely related animals. Very often, animals with poor vision are compensated by an excellent sense of smell and the reverse is also often true. Insects have very poor vision as regards detail, but this is offset in many of them by a tremendous field of view. A dragonfly can watch you as you walk around it without having to move head or eye, movements that in the field so often betray the presence of birds or mammals. Another important difference between our vision and that of insects lies in the useful range of the spectrum. Red light makes no impression on most insects, but they more than make up for this in the ultra-violet at the other end of the spectrum. We have seen that, in the early days of life on this earth, when insects were being evolved, ultra-violet was more plentiful than it is now. But what ultra-violet looks like to insects is anybody's guess.

When a stimulus is received at a sense organ, impulses spread through the nerves. A simple response may occur without reference to the brain, when it is called a reflex. When these changes do reach the brain they effect there other changes that endure. These are learning and memory. Complex considered responses are brought about by impulses passing out again from the brain to glands and muscles, usually many of them, the actions of which must be co-ordinated. For example, most of the muscles that operate the levers of the skeleton occur in antagonistic pairs; for any movement, one must relax while the other contracts.

The contraction of muscle is still not fully understood but it involves the reversible association of two fibrous proteins, actin and myosin, to a more complex protein, actomyosin (4). This appears to be by the sliding of alternate layers of the parallel fibres of these proteins into each other, much as the fingers may

74

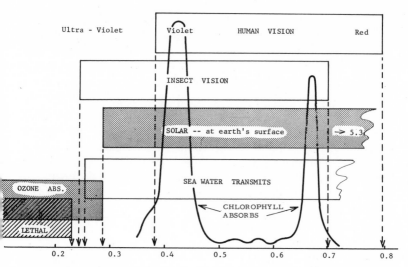

Figure 29. Life and the solar spectrum; the ozone layer shields life from lethal ultra violet.

be inter-locked in prayer. The force with which a muscle can contract depends on its thickness and may be over a thousand times its weight. Most muscles take about a tenth of a second for a complete contraction and relaxation. When nerve stimuli are received more frequently than this, the muscle remains contracted. Contractions of the special wing muscles of some very small insects, however, may follow each other a thousand times a second. This is perhaps the most striking thing about a muscle as a source of power, its versatility.

The end result of muscle contraction is behaviour, often movement to or from a congenial or uncongenial environment. Animals can swim, crawl, walk, run, leap, or fly with varying skill and agility. Leonardo da Vinci studied these mechanisms, especially the last in birds, and from them contrived devices calculated to carry a man into the air by his own muscular effort. This we have still not consistently achieved. His fellow countryman Borelli made further studies a hundred and fifty years later. More recent classical work in animal locomotion was that of Muybridge towards the end of the 19th century. This study was started in order to settle a bet as to whether a trotting horse ever has all four feet off the ground at one time (it does). It finally led to the invention of moving pictures; the motion picture industry has yet to acknowledge adequately its debt to students of animal locomotion. The number of ways in which an animal can walk or run depends on the number of legs it uses. When you swing your arms in walking—if you do—this is a vestige of the near-fore and off-hind gait of your quadrupedal ancestors.

We have seen that the forces muscles can exert depend on their sectional area, and the weights against which they must operate depend on the volume of the animal. The former increases as the square of the linear dimensions, the latter as the cube, so that the smaller an animal is the better it will be at weight lifting and at high jump in relation to its size. While we may do well to admire the performances of ants and grasshoppers in these events, man need apologize to no flea for his inability to jump over the Empire State building.

The evolution of the special senses has long been thought to have been closely associated with the development of the mind (5), and hence is perhaps of special interest to us with our inordinately large brains. Centralization of the nervous system in an animal implies memory and some learning ability. These are faculties we are beginning to understand; they enable past experience to influence future responses. The sum total of these responses, including those to stimuli from within the body comprise the behaviour of an animal, the basis of psychology. All this, of course, concerns the whole organism; it is here that physics and chemistry have not yet proved adequate.

And so we have travelled in company with these sciences as far as we can at present; we have reached the boundaries of physiology, where this study in the animal world nods acquaintance-ship with psychology the function of the mind, and where, in both plants and animals, it shakes hands with ecology, the study of organisms in relation to each other and to their environment, of organisms in communities.

7

LOVE ME,
LOVE
MY DOG

life in
the environment

Qui me amat, amet et canem meum.
ST. BERNARD,
In Festo Sancti Michaelis: Sermo Primus

Biological studies usually start out with the examination of a plant or an animal; they then proceed to dissect it, to take it to pieces and examine these, to see how the living thing was made up and to consider how it worked. Sooner or later, when we know enough about how plants and animals function, it becomes profitable to return to the whole plant and the whole animal and look at them again in the light of this knowledge, in relation to the surroundings in which they live. This means in relation not only to their physical and chemical surroundings, the climate and the weather, rocks, soil, and water, but also to their biological surroundings, other members of their own species, and other plants and animals living outside them or within them, in the same surroundings, parasites, predators, and associates, friends and foes in the living world.

This is the branch of biology that is known as ecology. It was given this name around 1870 by the German biologist, Ernst Haeckel; the name comes from the Greek *oikos* meaning 'home', and this is just what it deals with, plants and animals living at home. It is quite a new science; in fact perhaps the most recent branch of biology to achieve this status. But it has its roots back in the observations of the early naturalists and it owes much to these men. Modern biologists do well to look back often to the works of the early naturalists who observed more patiently than we and often commented with shrewder insight. Many a modern report, hailed as an epoch-making discovery, is naught but a rephrasing of old wisdom. Ecology then is sophisticated, scientific natural history. Like many young sciences it has been prolific of technical terms; we shall avoid these as far as possible, but perhaps I may be forgiven for using one here to illustrate this point: it is not for nothing that an ecologist has been defined as a man who calls a spade a geotome.

Let us take a look first of all at the physical and chemical surroundings of plants and animals, the environment or habitats in which they live. Most of you perhaps think you know about the weather, rocks and the soil, water, and so on already. But your knowledge will probably be from a human viewpoint. We need to take a closer look at these things from the viewpoints of plants and other animals, now that we know enough about these to appreciate their viewpoints.

Climate and its immediate manifestation, the weather, should be our first concern, since the more material surroundings like the soil are largely the outcome of the action of weather on rocks. The most important element of the weather is sunlight, or to use a broader term, including ultra-violet and infra-red and moonlight and starlight, radiation. Green plants are absolutely dependent on this, and most animals are absolutely dependent, directly or indirectly, on green plants. Sunlight is the ultimate source of nearly all the energy used by living things; and the amount of life that an area can support depends on the amount of radiation it receives. But less than one per cent of the energy the surface of the earth receives from the sun is used by plants in photosynthesis and hence finds its way into animal food supplies. Seas and lakes, with their algae and other aquatic plants are a little more efficient in this process than land surfaces. Of the rest of this radiant energy, much is lost back to outer space, much goes into the kinetic energy of winds and currents by the warming of air and water masses, much into the evaporation of water later returned as rain, and much into the maintenance of comfortable temperatures in the environments of plants and animals.

Temperature is, indeed, the next most important ingredient of the weather as far as life is concerned. You will realize of course that there is only a rather narrow range of temperature within which life can go on. You will realize too that animals fall into two groups as regards their body temperatures; warm-blooded animals, which control or regulate their temperatures at a constant level that is largely independent of outside changes; and cold-blooded animals, in which the body temperature conforms closely to the outside temperature—usually it is a little above this because of the heat of metabolism. Since the blood may be relatively warm or cold in either group, they are perhaps better described as the regulating animals and the conforming animals. Animals fall into two such groups in respect of other qualities besides temperature.

Obviously animals that can regulate their temperatures can carry on over a somewhat wider range than those that have to conform. The activity of all conformers is largely restricted to temperatures between the freezing point of water, 32° F., and about 130° F., the temperature of water a little too hot for you to get into. This gives a range of about a hundred fahrenheit degrees. Beyond both the upper and the lower limits of the temperature range for activity many conforming animals may survive in an inactive state. For example the larvae of some midges from African rock pools, which are subject to drying up, can survive dry temperatures up to 300° F., well above that of boiling water. Many insects that live during the winter in the arctic can withstand temperatures down to -30° F., and survival at -58° F. has been reported. So the survival range is more than three times the activity range.

At these extremes of temperature most animals contain less water than normal. At low temperatures animals get rid of water, just as you do from the radiator of your car, adding antifreeze instead. Incidentally, chemicals that you use as antifreeze are also to be found in some insects as an adaptation to low temperatures. At high temperatures even conforming animals can often cool themselves for a time by evaporating water.

Water evaporated from the seas returns to the earth's surface as rain, hail, and snow; we should consider these from the point of view of a small animal such as an insect. To us these things are a nuisance to be sure, and occasionally a hazard, but to small animals they may be catastrophic. One of the simplest properties of water, its surface tension, is barely perceptible to us; to many insects it is a force greater than their own weight and far greater

Figure 30.   Must match its whiteness.

than their tiny limbs can exert. Once entangled in this glutinous film an insect may remain a prisoner until evaporation or death releases it. On the wing or on the ground or vegetation, collision of small insects with raindrops several times their own size is certain death. A heavy rainstorm is one of the best controls for insects such as plant lice. And as for hail, imagine yourself out in the open with blocks of ice as big as cars falling thickly enough to cover the ground in a layer several cars deep. Snow is kind to most animals and plants, providing an insulating layer, which, if it comes abundantly and early enough, keeps temperatures in the upper layers of the soil, where many insects and plants pass the winter, well above the normal air temperatures. It is, of course, a conspicuous background for any dark-coloured animal, and many who remain active above it must match its whiteness.

One other factor needs mention, movement; winds in the air and the corresponding currents in water. These determine and limit much of the migration and dispersal of animals and some of the distribution of plants through pollination and seed dispersal. Wind and current may also carry the directional cues for the finding of food plant or host animal, mate or egg laying site. The primary cause of winds, too, is sunlight, through its effect on the temperature and barometric pressure of the air.

These components of climate are measured and recorded at weather stations, but the values obtained under the special standard conditions of these places are not necessarily those that relate to plant and animal life or activity. Wind speeds are greater on hills and in open country, less in valleys and woods or even on the lee side of a leaf. There are steep temperature gradients in the soil and in water, and warm-blooded animals provide halos of warmth around themselves, haven habitats for parasites on them, even when the weather man says it is thirty below. In a somewhat similar way the moisture transpired by plants may provide a humid halo around them much sought after by insects. These very local variations make up what is known as the microclimate and are of great interest to ecologists (2). Organisms are adept at finding favourable microclimates for themselves even in a very dismal weather picture.

The weather is not only of immediate interest to animals and plants but also of long-term indirect interest through the part

Figure 31.   The primary habitats . . . earth, water, air.

that it plays in moulding the crust of the earth, the principal place where animals and plants live. Rain and wind and temperature changes, especially repeated freezing and thawing, are the main agents of this process. In this way the habitats or living places are provided. Rock crumbles under the influence of rain and frost, a seed lodges in a crack, germinates and grows into a plant. The plant provides food for insects and a place for them to live, its roots crumble the rock further.

The primary habitats of plants and animals fall into three groups, earth, water, and air; although some of all three of these is necessary for life. The earth can be divided again into underground and surface habitats, and into desert and swamp or areas of stone, sand, or clay. The water can be divided into running and still; fresh, brackish and salt; liquid water and ice and snow, and of course, in all of these habitats the larger plants and animals provide specialized secondary habitats, both inside and outside themselves, for smaller plants and animals. These and other smaller specialized living places and the jobs that go with them the ecologist refers to as niches; a niche bears a similar relationship to the primary habitat with its community of organisms that a microclimate does to the weather.

A great many animals make special structures for themselves in their niches: burrows, nests, tubular cases, or webs. Some, like the white ants or termites and men, even provide their own microclimate by controlling the temperature and humidity within these homes to suit themselves. This seems reasonable in a conforming animal like a termite, but for man with his own efficient regulating system it seems like gilding the lily.

The air is a habitat with peculiarities of its own; so far as we know, no organisms live their lives entirely in the air, but a great many spend a large part of their time airborne. Most of these are very small forms or small reproductive stages of larger forms. Mites and small insects, pollen grains, and the spores of fungi and bacteria, are always to be found in the air up to several thousand feet above ground and sometimes in very large numbers. Some birds and bats and a few insects spend a large part of their time on the wing.

I have said that some contribution from each of the three major habitats, earth, water, and air, is necessary for life. It is for

Figure 32.   A five-foot thermostatic termite nest.

this reason that living things are most plentiful near the interfaces between two of these habitats; in the air and the vegetation near the surface of the ground or of water; in the ground near its surface, in the water near either of its surfaces. And they are, of course, most plentiful of all along the lines where all three habitats intersect; the shores of lakes, rivers, and seas. The last of these, the seashores, partly because of the effect of tides, are the most bountiful and fascinating habitat of all.

So far we have been talking mostly of the relations between organisms and their physical environment, the simple part of ecology. We now have to consider the relations of organisms with each other, with the biological part of their environment; and again we may take the simplest first, the relations between individuals of the same species; the relation between a spruce tree and its neighbouring spruce trees, an ant and other ants of the same species, a man and his neighbours. Most people recognize this social intercourse as a very important part of their own lives, but perhaps never even realize that it occurs in other organisms. Yet the mere fact that we find spruce trees, or poplars, or grasses in groups of a kind, that we have rabbit warrens and rookeries, flocks of geese and coveys of ducks, is a reflection of this social intercourse; of an elusive attraction that apparently exists between individuals of a species.

A special expression of this is the very specific attraction between the opposite sexes, with all the elaborate and sometimes bizarre colours and sounds, scents and dances that make up the courtship behaviour of animals. A further manifestation of it is found in family life, some measure of which may be shown even by quite primitive animals; indeed aggregations of animals may be the result in part of an incomplete dispersal of family groups, and in part of the fact that a site suitable for one individual is suitable for others of the same kind (2).

The intensity of aggregation varies tremendously, from the apparently almost solitary existence of many primitive and a few quite specialized animals, to the tightly knit, complex, highly organized societies of tens to hundreds of thousands of individuals found in some of the termites, bees, and ants. Since we have ourselves been making exceptionally rapid progress towards intensified social life, a closer look at this in other animals should be interesting to us.

There are a number of features found in nearly all of these highly organized societies (3).

Firstly, there are usually two or more different forms of individuals found in each colony; like the differences between the sexes in other animals these are adaptations to different functions, but the functions are social functions, not sexual functions. They may be associated with the different sexes, as the drone and the worker in honeybees, or they may be independent of sex, as the soldiers and the workers of termites. The number of each form or caste which a colony produces is not random, but determined by the needs of the colony.

Secondly, there are many peculiar feeding habits, the mutual sharing of food, which is swallowed and regurgitated and passed from one individual to another; vegetarianism in insects belonging to originally carnivorous groups; and what we can only call agriculture and animal husbandry, the growing of fungi and the herding of plant lice. These civilized habits of termites and ants are apparently related to the difficulty of obtaining sufficient animal food within range of a colony, for the large population that it contains. Man's agriculture, much later, had the same origin. And finally there is cannibalism as a means of population control when even vegetable food is insufficient. This last habit is a special case of a general subordination of the individual to the group, which often goes so far that individuals isolated from the colony are unable to survive.

A third group of features includes greatly improved communication between members of a colony, communication by sound, by scent, and by gesture; the control of temperature and other conditions inside the nest; and a tendency to indulge in battles with other colonies of the same species. This fighting seems to be in the nature of a substitution for the struggle for existence from which the individual insect is largely liberated by social life. This may be likened to what students of behaviour refer to as a displacement activity.

I would like to make just two points about these features. Firstly, if we represent the individual by a single cell and the colony by a complete animal of many cells, almost exact parallels to all of these features of social life are found on a simpler plane in a single animal. For example, the cells have different forms in different tissues; improved communication is represented by the nervous system and hormones, and battles within the species by cancer. This has given rise to the concept of a colony of social insects as a super-organism. Secondly, these features are so constant in other groups of social animals, and so strangely suggestive of many features of human history that the resemblance can hardly be accidental. I shall return to this point in my last chapter.

The relations between different species are endlessly varied (4). In any particular habitat, there will be found one or more communities of plant and animal species that are related to each other as food and feeder, the eaten and the eater. There may be, in one and the same habitat, separate communities active at different seasons of the year, or even at different times of the day and night. The chains of predator-prey relationships, often called food chains, usually have some six or seven links in them. The first link, of course, is a plant, a primary producer of carbohydrate. Thereafter the successive links are usually animals of progressively greater size, since predators usually prey on animals smaller than themselves. There may be more than one kind of predator feeding on a particular prey and more than one kind of prey taken by a particular predator. So that food chains may branch and reunite, when a food web results. The classical example of this sort of connection used by Charles Darwin, but improved by others, attributes the glory of England to her maiden ladies. The yeomen of England are fattened on roast beef from cattle fed on clover, which is pollinated by bumble-bees, which are preyed on by mice, which are eaten by cats kept by maiden ladies.

In a straightforward food chain, since the successive links are larger animals, it follows that they must be present in smaller numbers and that they must reproduce more slowly. The earlier links must reproduce fast enough to maintain their own populations and to provide a surplus to nourish the next link. Each successive link in the sequence, plant, herbivore, carnivore, must represent progressively less of the original energy of sunlight put into the system. Usually it also includes both a smaller number of individuals and a smaller weight of living material. These

Darwin's food chain

Figure 33.   Darwin's food chain (D.A. Burns).

Figure 34. The predator-prey relationship; two links in a food chain. (Note the toad's inflation, making swallowing difficult.)

pyramid effects, the pyramid of energy and the pyramid of numbers, are useful in understanding what goes on in a plant and animal community. The final predator at the top of the pyramid may die of old age, assisted perhaps by disease, parasites, or scavengers. These and the micro-organisms of decay return the living material to a lower level of the pyramid, converting part of it all the way back to plant nutrients in the soil.

A predator lives on the capital of its prey, while a parasite, or at least a good parasite, lives only on the interest. A good parasite does not kill its host but keeps it alive for the benefit of its offspring. Unlike predators, parasites are nearly always both smaller and more numerous than their hosts, but they too may be links in a food chain; there may be parasites on parasites, and parasites in parasites. These food chains or food webs collectively resemble an inverse pyramid of numbers. Most of the micro-organisms of disease are among the smallest and most numerous of parasites but they are too often fatal to their hosts to be looked upon as good parasites.

True parasites take all their food from their hosts to whom they contribute nothing. But by no means all the relations between different species of plants and animals are antagonistic; nature is full of examples of everything from competition, through friendly rivalry and tolerance or commensalism, to elaborate associations for mutual benefit. Animals or plants may compete for nesting sites, root space, sunlight, food, mates, or anything that the environment provides. In competition between species extinction is usually the price of failure; competition is a major factor in evolution. Many animals attach themselves to others but get only transport or protection from them: the barnacles on a whale or for that matter on the ships of man. Others, like the sea anemones and hermit crabs, which occupy respectively the outside and the inside of the disused shells of marine snails, have a more complex relationship; the anemone feeds on the crab's leavings, and affords it a measure of protection with its stinging cells. Finally, in the lichens we have a

Figure 35.   Lichens . . . necessary associations between algae and fungi.

necessary association between a green photosynthetic alga providing food and a fungus providing moisture, neither of which can survive alone.

Two other aspects of ecology must be briefly mentioned. I have referred to the part played by winds and ocean currents in the dispersal of plants and animals. Despite this and the extensive movements, migrations and random movements under their own volition, plants and animals are far from being uniformly distributed. There are, for example, no snakes in Ireland, and no native mammals save bats in New Zealand. The careful study of facts of this sort, biogeography, can tell us a great deal not only about the evolution, migration, and dispersal, of plants and animals, but also about the history of the earth, especially with regard to the distribution of land masses. And the more we learn about migrations, especially the long-range periodic movements of many birds, and some fish and insects, the more intriguing this becomes, with its revelations of route-finding ability and phenomenal powers of perception, interpretation, and endurance.

It is obvious that ecology is important to an understanding of the factors that control the size of populations. The most striking facts to emerge from this study are: firstly, that populations of animals vary much less in complex communities of many species than in simple ones of a few species—diversity means stability (5); secondly, that the variations of population often show a somewhat irregular periodicity, sometimes referred to as population cycles. The study of variations in populations, or population dynamics, is most readily pursued with insects because of their small size and short life cycles. Can we extrapolate from these studies to our own population problems? Since a pest may be defined as a species that is overly abundant, and a problem crop is one that is not abundant enough, it is clear that ecology is important as a basis for applied biology.

8

SEASON
OF
MISTS

applications
of biology

Season of mists and mellow
fruitfulness,
Close bosom-friend of the
maturing sun . . .
KEATS, *To Autumn*

So far, I have been discussing biology for its own sake; the
ultimate science for its own sake. But it is in the nature of animals
to make use of what they learn and man is no exception. The
applications of biological knowledge in agriculture and medicine
and animal husbandry, in forestry and geography and ocean-
ography, and, it is to be hoped, in cosmology and astronautics,
represent such a profusion of fruitfulness that most people lose
sight of the original and basic science on which these depend, if
indeed they ever had a glimpse of it. For this reason I propose
to content myself with some brief comments on applied biology,
on what some of these vast fields of knowledge—and ignorance—
look like from below, from the level of their foundations.

It is usually held that the principal fields in which biological
knowledge is applied are agriculture and medicine, each interpreted in the broadest sense. But there is really no limit to the
fields in which biological knowledge proves useful, and perhaps
its most important application is to be found in the daily life of
each and every one of us.

Hitherto the most productive field of application has been in
agriculture, where, assisted of course by chemistry and physics,
the fruitfulness of the earth has been increased manifold. But the
history of these developments is littered with tragedies—rabbits
in Australia, water hyacinth choking many of the world's great
rivers, European corn borer taking its toll in North America.

Many of these tragedies have been the outcome of good intentions; many more of ignorance and stupidity. Biology is not a science to be trifled with; a sound, thorough knowledge of a wide field of the science is a necessary preliminary to application. Biological knowledge needs to be mellowed in experience with varied environments before it is applied. Attempts have too often been made to apply raw and limited information that proves to be at variance with basic principle, with unhappy consequences. Too often the long view has been neglected in the interests of short-term gain. The world structure of agriculture is top heavy, lacking in the foundations of basic knowledge that make for soundness; and the support for the medical sciences is not much better. This is the natural outcome of the dependence of research on commercial interests, which are usually of a rather short-term nature, for financial support. The fault lies in governments and universities, which should be able to see the necessity for foundations and to take the long-term view, but which have nevertheless allowed this to happen.

We spend, for example, millions of dollars learning how to grow better potatoes, but deny a few hundred thousand to the systematic field work that might discover for us something altogether better than potatoes, a new, as yet undescribed species; thousands of man-hours have gone into breeding fatter cattle, while millions of other animals, any one of which could have unsuspected uses, remain unknown to man. And while nearly one-half of the applied biologists are trying to apply inadequate basic knowledge to increasing the world's supply of food and fibre so that there may be more for everybody, the other half supports the medical professions in their efforts to keep more and more people alive for longer and longer so that there shall be less for everybody. At the same time, commercial interests, aided and abetted by governments, guided no doubt by sound economic principles, if not by biological ones, buy up and destroy or hoard the surpluses that one-half of the world has striven to produce but does not want, and that the other half is dying for but cannot afford.

Much of the activity of applied biologists can be resolved into population control—upwards for the desirable species, crops, forest trees, livestock, game animals; downwards for the undesirable

Figure 36. Potatoes and populations; some nineteenth century movements.

species, pests, weeds, disease micro-organisms, and other parasites, and in days gone by, beasts of prey. Much of the difficulty lies in deciding which group an animal belongs in, whether a plant is harmful or beneficial, and, finally, what we mean by harmful and beneficial, by good and bad. A species beneficial in one circumstance may be harmful in another, and certainly goodness at one population level may be badness at another. Overcrowding is the most important single factor in epidemics of all kinds. We have defined a pest as a species that is overly abundant; but I think it takes two to make a pest. Two species, both overly abundant.

To illustrate a number of these points, I can hardly do better than tell the story of the Irish, the potato, the fungus *Phytophthora infestans*, which causes late blight in this important crop, and the potato beetle, *Leptinotarsa decemlineata*. The Irish, as you know, are great potato eaters, and in the early years of the last century the principal crop in Ireland and the principal item in the diet of Irishmen was the potato. A large population of potatoes supported a large and growing population of Irishmen.

About 1830, another species came on the scene, late blight fungus from South America, the original home of the potato. This, like all fungi, has no chlorophyll; it must live a parasitic life, in this instance, on the potato. In the favourable Irish potato population it multiplied at the expense of the potatoes until by 1845 there were crop failures, and famine, and emigration of Irishmen to North America (1).

All this time, a rare, rather pretty, yellow-and-black-striped beetle munched unobtrusively on wild relatives of the potato in the Middle West. It was doubtless unaware of the magnificent future before it. The influx of Irishmen increased the demand for potatoes, which was met by extending their cultivation westwards into the range of our yellow and black beetle. Pure crop potatoes provided suitable food plants in fabulous profusion. The population of this beetle proved no less sensitive to changes in the population of potatoes than did the Irishmen before it. It became a pest of the first magnitude; its population pressure pushed it into the eastern states with such impetus that it boarded ships and was introduced into Europe to play havoc with what late blight had left of potato crops there.

And so we see that our own population, its magnitude and its movements, is influenced by the populations of a seed plant, a fungus, and a beetle. This should remind us that, although man need no longer fear any other animal, at least while he remains in his own habitats and carries arms when outside them, this does not mean that he can afford to ignore other plants and animals.

In man's earlier days he grew up close to nature, he inherited instincts that told him how he should behave towards most of the species he encountered. Today, most of us bring up our children in a biological vacuum. Our homes are sterile and our schools nearly so. In this safe environment the old instincts are lost and each of us has to learn afresh to live with life. Failing this we carry forward into adulthood an attitude of obliviousness to, or at best disregard for other organisms, which culminates in the ludicrous view of ourselves as being in no sense animals, but rather—little gods; a dangerous doctrine, indeed.

The advantages of hygiene and cleanliness are real enough, certainly to the soap manufacturers, but they do pose other problems, both medical and educational. Poliomyelitis is no problem in unhygienic countries where people develop immunity to it in their tender years. In a sterile school, children have to learn about biology from books and pictures, instead of learning it by contact with living plants and animals. The best way to learn which end of a bee stings is the scientific way of hypothesis and experiment. Such knowledge endures.

I would like now to turn again to the Colorado potato beetle and consider what has been done about it. In the middle years of last century men reached into their poison grab-bag and pulled out an arsenical poison that had been used for centuries against tyrants, rich uncles, and mothers-in-law: Paris green. Obviously this is a versatile poison, and it killed beneficial insects just as dead as it killed rich uncles and potato beetles. Today, a hundred years later, what do we do? I quote from a recent textbook (2): 'Control is accomplished by applying dusts of five per cent DDT' or 'a one-to-three mixture of calcium arsenate and hydrated lime'. An arsenical poison again; but as first choice an even less discriminate poison, DDT; such is progress. No biological problem was ever yet satisfactorily solved by chemistry.

It is surprising that the Colorado potato beetle has not developed resistance to this group of insecticides after they have been used against it for a hundred years. This phenomenon of resistant strains is now such a common one in many fields of applied biology, in both medicine and agriculture, that we may pause to look at its causes. The resistance of insects to insecticides is not a new thing. It was first reported shortly before the turn of the century, and was predicted earlier still. It is in fact, as old as evolution. Plants evolved components poisonous to insects quite early in their history. Insects of today that feed on these plants have been selected for resistance to these components.

In an earlier chapter I referred to the variation that all species show in most of their attributes and to how this was caused. The susceptibility of the individuals of a species to poisons varies; some are much more susceptible than others and at either end of the curve of variation there is a long tail representing on the one hand a few individuals that are very susceptible, and on the other a few that are very resistant. When we apply an insecticide to a crop, or administer a drug to a patient suffering from a disease caused by a micro-organism, we place the insect or the micro-organism in an environment that selects for survival those few very resistant individuals. For economic reasons, or because of the risk of damaging the crop or poisoning the patient, it is rarely practicable to use poisons at the very high doses needed to kill every last individual. These survivors proceed to breed. They raise another generation like themselves, the fittest to survive in this new environment that we provide. It is possible by selecting in this way, experimentally, to develop strains of insects that require thousands of times the normal dosage of a poison to kill them—obviously no longer an economic proposition.

In the field of insect control we now have strains of large numbers of pests that can no longer be economically killed with many of the poisons discovered within the last fifteen years. Travelling in Africa today, it is necessary to know, for each area one visits, to what anti-malarial drugs the local strains of malaria parasites have developed resistance so that one may select one that will still afford protection. This phenomenon, of course, is nothing more or less than evolution by natural—or unnatural—selection, convincing evidence of the truth and the significance of this process. Fatally convincing; patients die if treated only with a drug to which their strain of parasite is resistant.

There are then two key problems in reducing the too large population, firstly to kill only the species in question, and secondly to circumvent the development of resistant strains. For the first, where the use of drugs and poisons is essential, we need to know much more about the biochemistry and the genetics of the organisms we seek to control, and also about the mode of action of the drugs and poisons we plan to use against them. It may then be possible to do some chemical tailoring of our poisons to make them much more specific, so that they will kill one species and one only. We have already seen that species are chemically distinct in their DNA, the basis of genetic material, and structurally distinctive in their numbers of chromosomes.

What about resistant strains? For this purpose we will need to tailor a second chemical, also specific, which acts in a different way to the first. Resistance of the victim to the first must be linked with susceptibility to the second. The first material will then select for survival the progenitors of a strain more and more resistant to itself, but more and more susceptible to the second.

At a suitable stage of resistance the switch will be made to the second material, which will then select back a strain susceptible to the first. By using two such materials alternately it should be possible to extend their usefulness many times.

These are primarily chemical remedies. Until our chemistry reaches this advanced level, control of insects with poisons, in nature at least, should be restricted to emergency situations and when all else fails. It is a crude procedure and a counsel of despair; its use is evidence of bankruptcy of ideas.

What other recourse have we? The possibilities are as numerous as the species of insects. Man differs from insects principally in his intellectual ability. He needs to use this to learn about the biology and especially the natural history and ecology of species that trouble him or his crops. He should then be able to restore the situation by subtle manipulation of the environment, the friends and foes of his subject of study, even the genetics of the subject itself (3). He may need to grow something different, or grow the crop in a different place, or select from it a strain resistant to the pest. Often a study of the circumstances that brought about a pest situation will suggest a simple way in which it may be terminated. Sometimes, when there is a conflict of interests between man and some other animal, I think man needs, with due humility, to consider his own ways and ask whether he is not himself at fault.

We have seen that high populations are the essence of pest problems, and that diversity of species means stability of specific populations. It follows that anything that tends to impoverish the flora and fauna of an area, as many of man's activities including pest control procedures do, will in the long run but aggravate pest problems.

Man, since he became pastoral, has become very stuffy in his eating habits, and even in the other uses that he makes of plants and animals, and their products. Diversifying crops and animal food would solve many problems. If you cannot control a weed or an insect in any other way you can always eat it, either first hand or through the intermediary of some other animal that likes it better.

To take just one example, the white ants or termites are regarded as among the more important insect pests of tropical and subtropical regions. They are palatable and highly nutritious insects providing a well-balanced meal rich in high-grade protein (4). They need little food besides cellulose, wood pulp or paper, which they convert into assimilable form more efficiently than any other animal. Many species are easy to rear. It is believed that, in the past in Africa, they have enabled man to survive through periods of shortage of other proteins, and incidentally that man's first use of tools was in opening their cantankerous nests. Many tribes relish them today. In this world drowning in paper, news-less newspapers, examination papers,

Figure 37. Termite damage to a tent.

and endless forms-in-triplicate, what a godsend these insects could be. The spectacle of our editors and advertisers, professors and politicians, eating their words for breakfast would be some compensation for the inroads made into our pulpwood forests. All the trees are, after all, directly or indirectly, bread and cheese, or at least our only ultimate source of carbohydrate. I think we must look upon all organisms as being potentially beneficial, even to the somewhat narrow interests of man, and only a very few as truly detrimental.

One cannot but feel some sympathy with Lord Dunsany, an

Irishman, perhaps influenced by the history of the potato, who wrote:

When man has poisoned all the flowers
And stilled the insects' glee,
Our fields with chemistry,
And killed the birds with spray that showers
In his well regulated bowers,
How lonely man will be.

We have seen that the general effect of advances in the applications of biology in medicine has been that more people live longer. There are a few special effects that need mention. Who are these people who live longer? Who survive when they might have died? They include a higher than usual proportion of people who by earlier criteria, the criteria of nature in the raw, would have been found unfit for survival. But this does not necessarily mean, as people have suggested, a general deterioration of the human race. It does mean a change in the meaning of fitness: these people are as fit to survive in the new environment as they were unfit in the old. And it also means a change in the rate of human evolution, a kind of biological stagnation.

Two other special effects that may possibly offset this, the antagonistic developments of artificial insemination and birth control, have both been on the one hand hailed as the saviours of the race and on the other damned as monstrous and inhuman. These much discussed procedures have an obvious bearing on one of our central problems, that of population, but this bearing is neither so simple nor so direct as is commonly supposed. Birth control is often viewed as the answer to the population problem, but unless it were enforced, which is hardly possible, it is a self-limiting process. Those who find it an acceptable answer and practice it, automatically become fewer in each succeeding generation. Both birth control and artificial insemination can however restore some of the flexibility to human evolution. They are among the more important means by which genetical knowledge can be applied to the improvement of the human species—eugenics. When we have sufficient genetical knowledge (5).

The stability of populations that comes with diversity of species is only one of its advantages. There are but few species of plant or animal that man knows so well that he can condemn them as wholly bad. That is, few that we should get rid of if we could. Too often one hears the cry: 'Eradicate!'. This word means, of course, to root out, and if used at all it should be restricted to plants. As far as insects are concerned we have not yet been able to eliminate any species, at least not when we have wanted to. It is one of the strange paradoxes of life that when an animal is in danger of extinction, man's best efforts have often failed to save it, but when it is a question of getting rid of some other species this seems to thrive. Perhaps this is the true measure of the success of our conquest of nature, of our ability as a species on comparison with others. It seems likely that man has contributed towards the extinction of more other species of plants and animals than any other organism. He has not, as yet, shown himself capable of replacing them. As a general principle, it is unwise to do that which one cannot undo, or rather to unmake that which one cannot make.

The now widely publicized objectives of conservation come close to this objective of diversity of organisms but hardly close enough. I think we need to look rather carefully at the objectives of conservation. Too often they are directed exclusively, or at least predominantly at animals of known and immediate interest to man, game animals, fish and fowl, not at life in general. Some of those who shout loudest 'Conserve those trout!' may be heard to add under their breath: 'Keep them alive and swimming until I can get there and get them on a hook!'. Too often I have seen a mere 200 or so pounds of conservationist, riding to a meeting on conservation in two and a half tons of car, burning fuel at a rate that would make Old Nick envious. We should not forget that coal and oil are a biological legacy from plants of past ages and that we are living on capital in our use of them. Conservation gets lip service, in two senses; when it suits us.

We measure progress in terms of gross national product or standard of living; but what does a gross nation produce besides its standard of living? And at what price does it produce this, in terms of resources? Would North Americans not do better to take a slice off their standard of living, bringing it a little more into line with the world average, and to devote the proceeds towards raising the standard of learning? The next generation will be bigger than ours; they too may need some resources.

We have seen that life in the sea converts the energy of sunlight into food more efficiently than that on the land even under our most intensive agriculture. Since seven tenths of the earth's surface is water, marine biology must receive more attention and aquaculture must supplement and may perhaps replace agriculture. A temporary reprieve from starvation may be thus secured, by returning to where life started from for our food supplies. Perhaps in this area we shall have a chance to learn from our mistakes on land, but only if we start now to concern ourselves more seriously about the effects some of these may have in the ocean.

We see then that the solution of one problem in applied biology, as often as not creates another. Sometimes two others. The problems created may be less serious, but then our standards

Figure 38. Sea harvest; returning to where life started from for our food supplies.

become more exacting. The applied biologist's job is thus self-perpetuating, a happy situation for him, if uneconomic for society. I see this as a reflection of the point with which I started out: the applications of biology are houses built upon sand; the foundations of pure science on which they rest are inadequate to carry the load. Man has been trying too much to mould the rest of the natural world to his wishes without adequate understanding of the laws that govern it. He needs, in his own interests, to acquire a better comprehension of these laws and then to see how best he can adapt his needs to what the rest of the natural world can do for him. Less take and more give. As Carlyle put it: 'If you will have your laws obeyed without mutiny, see well that they be pieces of God Almighty's Law; otherwise, all the artillery in the world will not keep down mutiny'.

9

MASTER
OF
MY FATE

where do we
go from here?

I am the master of my fate:
I am the captain of my soul.
W. E. HENLEY,
Echoes, iv. Invictus. In Mem. R.T.H.B.

We like to think that we, the human species, know where we are going, that we control our future. This idea can be refuted with two examples. The first step towards a new generation, we refer to as falling in love, an expression that reflects our lack of control over this very personal biological process. For at least a century most people have held the opinion that war is bad, that we should not fight, that the money it costs could be better spent. And yet in the last century there have been two major 'hot' wars, a long-drawn-out cold one, and almost continuous minor ones. We have no more control over national hatreds than over personal loves. Does it not look as though 'Things are in the saddle and ride mankind'?

Many people have attempted to define the causes of war, ascribing them to political ambition, relationships between populations and food supply and land space, historical antecedents, and economic factors. Bernard Shaw claimed that war began when the interest on capital fell to two and a half per cent and ceased when the destruction had lifted it back to five per cent. But these things are no more causes of war than pulling a trigger is a cause of murder. To find the basic cause we need to go much deeper into man's biological history. Herbert Spencer (1) and Charles Darwin spoke of the struggle for existence and the survival of the fittest. This is a struggle in which living matter has been engaged for ten thousand times as long as man has been in existence. May we not expect that the necessity to struggle has, in this time, become in some way built into the behaviour of organisms? We have seen that organized social life protects the individual from—or perhaps it would be better to say, robs the individual of—the necessity for struggle, at least in its juvenile stages. Such instinct, such built-in behaviour cannot just be turned off, however; in the society it finds its expression in battles between colonies of the same species—in, for example, termites, and bees and ants and, I submit, in the wars of man. Small wonder that man has difficulty in controlling war, a displacement activity for the struggle for existence.

Looked at in this light, it would seem that our best hope for progress towards peace would lie in substituting some other challenge, some other struggle of similar magnitude, for that of which our recent evolution has robbed us; a double displacement activity. With the problem of population versus food supply in mind, a possibility that suggests itself is space travel and the colonization of other planets. Here surely is a challenge worthy of our mettle. The East/West cold war would appear in its true colors of stupidity from the heat of Venus, if both sides together faced the challenge of establishment there. As overcrowding in the sea led to invasion of the land and overcrowding of the land to invasion of the air, overcrowding of this planet may well force adaptation to another. In a project of this sort other species than man will be needed; perhaps those very pests that we are trying to eradicate from the earth. Our survival on the earth is dependent on our plant and animal associates; our establishment in such a foreign environment would be doubly so (2).

I think the final value of living things for each other and for man is the educational value. To gain control over our destiny seems to be one clear human objective; those who disagree are those who think we already have it. The fundamental obstacle to this control is ignorance in biology, especially of genetics, human genetics and its application to human improvement, eugenics. Among the many wisdoms of Malthus is this: 'Every point of nature seems peculiarly calculated to furnish stimulants to mental exertion . . . inexhaustible food for the most unremitted enquiry'. Biology demands a place as a compulsory subject in our school curricula. To deny the next generation a full treatment of biology in their education is to risk denial of a future to humanity. What really matters is that those who control our destinies, our governments and politicians, have a background of biological knowledge. It may be that a required course in ecology and population dynamics as a condition for holding government office would serve. But since a healthy democracy requires a public no less well educated than its leaders, universal instruction in biology seems to me essential. How can we hope to understand what is happening to us as a species without this training? And how can we hope for even a measure of control over our destiny without this understanding? A little knowledge is indeed a dangerous thing, but less may well be catastrophic.

I have said a measure of control advisedly. It will always be necessary for man to recognize his animal nature and to live within the boundaries set by the organic world. He may be able, in co-operation with other organisms, to play a part in extending these boundaries, both in space as I have said, and in time. For it must be assumed that life has boundaries in time; we have discussed its beginnings, about which we know something and can learn more; it must surely have an end, about which we may only speculate. Human life began but recently, its end may be imminent; our only hope of having any say about this lies in an investment in biological knowledge. There are animals in existence, lamp shells in the sea, that have been around without change of genus for about 400 million years; other kinds have had but a brief career. In general, plants and animals with few special attributes, the all-rounders of the living world, have endured longest. Many of the dinosaurs, with the special feature of enormous bulk, had but a brief span of life. Man is specialized. He has an enormous brain . . . Before we bow our way off the stage of life we might give a thought to how our record will be written. Are we to go down in the pages of biological history as the greatest destroyer of other species and the only one to consider itself superior to the laws of nature? Or can we accomplish something better than this? We must first agree on what our objectives are to be (3).

In the struggle for existence most organisms reproduce on a scale far beyond the numbers that can survive. This was the Malthusian seed that germinated into the tree of evolution in the mind of Darwin. Man, although largely released from this struggle for existence, continues to reproduce rapidly. Despite wide recognition of the conflict between population increase and the limitations of food supply, population continues to increase and indeed most national policies are still directed at this (4). Most governments, too, strive for improved standards of living. These objectives are essentially those expressed by the Italian thinker Beccario as long ago as 1764: 'the greatest happiness of the greatest number'. Jeremy Bentham echoed this as 'the greatest good for the greatest number' in 1798, a strange year to choose, for it was the year of publication of Malthus's essay on population, and both Beccario and Bentham meant, of course, the greatest number of men. It is strange because Malthus demonstrates so clearly that a contradiction can be found in this phrase. Feed men, and they reproduce; their 'greatest good' leads to their greater number. We cannot have both the greatest good and the greatest number, only the greatest good *or* the greatest number.

As Malthus pointed out, great numbers will mean great misery; population control by famine, pestilence, and war. The assumption on which Malthus based his 'dismal theorem' was that population would increase geometrically, food supply only arithmetically. But what is food supply save the poulation increase of our food plants and animals, which is geometrical? That food supply does not in fact increase geometrically is at present due to human laziness, or ineptitude, or biological ignorance. It may eventually be due to land shortage, or sea shortage.

In any event, if more and more men seemed a poor thing as a human objective to Malthus, it seems poorer still today. And the objective of higher and higher standards of living is clearly incompatible with it. I would like to rephrase Beccario's dictum by changing the last word, to encompass the arguments I have put forward for the maintenance of a diversity of species: 'the greatest good of the greatest number of *species*'. This, I submit, is a worthy objective for man; it has of course implications for human population, to which I shall return.

Let me first consider the alternative objective, a continuing build-up of human populations, which many people still seem to consider desirable. The world can, of course, support a much larger human population than it does now, but at what price?

Larger populations will mean progressively more intense social organization. In other animals, especially the social insects, these circumstances have led to vegetarianism, to communism in the original sense of the word, the subordination of the individual to the group, and, as a special case of this, to cannibalism. And finally to anatomical differences between these individuals, to the formation of workers and soldiers and queens and to battles between colonies of the same species. There is reason to believe that similar consequences might be expected in man. There would be no more T-bone steaks; we should not be able to afford the inefficiencies of eating our plants second hand—maximum food per acre is to be obtained in the plant form. Communism, cannibalism, and the anatomical specialization of people for particular functions; for breeding, for brain work, and for brawn work, the last perhaps specifically for more wars to end wars.

But the biggest price to pay would be the sacrifice of other species. Inevitably, as population goes up, a greater and greater proportion of the world's surface will be taken up by our habitations and by areas devoted to production for our ever more elaborate desires, until little will remain for any other species save those we think we need. And each one that goes, goes for good. Hunting and fishing as pastimes will go early. National parks are already threatened; even a walk or a drive in the country would be incompatible with this objective. Intensive agriculture everywhere. These changes will not take place without a struggle; pest problems and some disease problems will be rapidly aggravated. It may well be that a balance will be struck, a truce arranged between man and the rest of nature. Would it not become us to arrange this early, rather than have it forced upon us late?

How many of us, then, should there be? What is an optimum population for man? I would put this at one billion, rather less than a third of our present population. I base this figure on the fact that this was approximately the world population in the middle of the last century, and that it was at that time that man's agriculture first began to fall foul of other organisms, especially insects. True, there were agricultural pests before that time, locusts and the like, which breed elsewhere than in crops; but the real problems, the story of the potato beetle and countless others like it, date from around the middle of the nineteenth century. I am convinced that if we could return to this level of population many of our problems would disappear. In further support of this figure, a billion people uniformly distributed over the habitable areas of the world would give an average density roughly the same as the present average density in the inhabited areas of Canada.

These questions of population have political implications. Governments influence population trends, but mostly upwards. As recently as 1944, a Royal commission was appointed in Britain to investigate the failure of the population to grow: this was wartime. And in Canada a recent high-level conference on renewable resources spent much of its time discussing human resources, apparently concerned over the shortage of us. Canada could be repopulated ten times over from the low countries in Europe, from India, or from China. Those who urge larger populations on the world should live for a spell in these countries.

Surely, now that we are sending patrols into outer space we can start to look beyond our own national boundaries and consider these problems at home on a world-wide basis. We may question whether our own politicians have the knowledge this calls for, the biological knowledge, even the demographic knowledge. I do not think demographers anywhere are satisfied with the data at present provided by censuses, data on which population forecasts depend. This is a matter that any government could easily remedy. A biologist cannot but wonder whether the government of South Africa appreciates the biological implications of its policy of apartheid. It is an attempt to legislate reproductive isolation between colour groups. But, reproductive isolation is a requirement for the evolution of species. It is thus an attempt, perhaps unwitting, to divide *Homo sapiens* into two species, a black and a white. A few minutes in South Africa are sufficient to show what little success this has had.

I have referred briefly to cannibalism. This is such a logical way of controlling surplus population that I would like to consider it a little further. It is the only procedure that can fill a dual role in the population-versus-food-supply problem; at one and the same time it reduces the population and augments the food supply. It is a very common phenomenon among other animals; most animals that are omnivorous, like man, will resort to it under just such conditions as those that man now approaches. Usually the young are eaten, those animals that are not yet of reproductive age, and it is a common fate of males after mating.

Please do not mistake me here; I am not recommending a return to cannibalism. I am suggesting that as population increases our attitude towards this custom may be expected to change. There are parts of Africa and the Far East where it is not uncommon, and it has apparently been increasing in the Congo. Is it, after all, any less ethical than war? As the number of living persons increases, our concern about deaths will inevitably decrease. From a biological viewpoint our concern should be for selectiveness in mortality.

From death we might pass on and consider what biology has to say about immortality, about life after death. We have seen that single-celled plants and animals reproducing by division are possessed of this doubtful blessing inherently. They are subject only to accidental death. In many-celled animals this property is restricted to the germ cells, the eggs and the sperm, of which the favoured few achieve immortality, or at least another lifetime, through fertilization. A man lives on in his children; but he also lives on in his works, in the effects that he has on his environment. From the ecological viewpoint every animal, through its activities in contact with other animals, and especially through those that it eats and is eaten by, leaves a legacy of influence extending indefinitely into the future, which is its immortality, its life after death. In this sense, men, with their buildings and works of art and writings, have a greater measure of immortality than other animals.

If one looks on the soul as the immortal part of an animal then a biologist must regard it as a sort of synthesis of the genes of the germ cells on the one hand, and the sum total of the influences on the environment on the other. The soul has meant many things to many people; it makes some rather interesting appearances in the history of biological thought. The French philosopher René Descartes held that man differed from all other animals in the possession of a soul. This he considered was located in a small structure in the brain, the pineal body, which in his day was known to occur only in man. It is now known to occur in all vertebrates and to represent a vestigial eye, which was well developed in many fossil vertebrates, and is well developed still in one living lizard. This eye is truly the mirror of the soul!

Should we then assume that all vertebrates have souls? John Ray, the seventeenth-century English parson-naturalist, in his book *The Wisdom of God Manifested in the Works of the Creation* published in 1691, ascribed the development of form in both plants and animals to the soul: 'the Operator in the formation of the Bodies of Man and other Animals . . . The sensitive Soul itself'. Fifty years earlier Thomas Browne in his *Religio Medici,* referring to the changes of form of insects, wrote: 'These strange and mystical transmigrations that I have observed in silkworms turned my Philosophy into Divinity . . . Who wonders not at the operation of two souls in those little Bodies?'—one soul for the caterpillar, and one for the moth. The metamorphosis of insects is, as we have seen, controlled by hormones; the pineal body too produces a hormone. The soul, as these men saw it, is now resolved into a hormone, a chemical messenger: obviously this is a somewhat different meaning from that which the word carries today. It seems to me preposterous to deny a soul, however this may be defined, to a dog that dies saving the life of a child, to a horse that may think for its rider, while according this doubtful privilege to all men regardless.

Much has been made of the supposed conflict between religion and science, especially biology. Narrow viewpoints in either field make ready conflicts with the other. The more familiar one becomes with this living world, the more one comes to marvel at its intricate subtleties and wonder at its awesome scale. If these are not religious feelings then I am mistaken in my understanding of the word.

Most men of goodwill now accept an allegorical interpretation of the biblical account of the creation, but there remains a divergence between the Bible and biology which we need to be reminded of. We read in Genesis: 'And the fear of you and the dread of you shall be upon every beast of the earth and upon every fowl of the air; with all wherewith the ground teemeth, and all the fishes of the sea, into your hand they are delivered. Every moving thing that liveth shall be food for you; as the green herb have I given you all.' An early and courageous challenge to this attitude came from John Ray who wrote in 1691: 'Let us then consider the works of God and admire His infinite goodness and wisdom in the formation of them. No creature in the sublunary world is capable of doing this except man, and yet we have been deficient therein.' Alexander Pope went further a generation later:

Know, Nature's children all divide her care;
The fur that warms a monarch, warm'd a bear.
While Man exclaims, 'See all things for my use!'
'See man for mine!' replies a pamper'd goose;
And just as short of reason he must fall,
Who thinks all made for one, not one for all.

This viewpoint has grown apace as man's struggle against competing organisms for survival has waned; now that his struggle for survival is with himself it is held by men of many faiths and by men of none. Old Testament dogma here conflicts with modern ecology as well as with Christian charity. If man is to survive, it will not be alone.

Biologists who view a man as something apart from all other organisms, calling for a special science for which I have coined the term neosymbology, draw their arguments from the philosophy of Descartes. This view has arisen through looking for somewhere to draw the line in allocating souls, and the most conspicuous break to man is, naturally, that nearest to him. It would seem that in this view, the gulf between man and, say, gorilla is greater than that between gorilla and amoeba. The argument still rests chiefly on differences of a rather abstract character and especially on communication, including the use of symbols, writing, and the accumulation of knowledge from generation to generation. This is called cultural evolution, as distinct presumably from wild or uncultivated evolution, implying that man controls it. I have already discussed this claim.

It was but recently that von Frisch (5) unravelled the meaning of the dance symbolism with which honeybees communicate; and similar as yet unintelligible intricacies have since been found in the lives of ants and other social insects. Animals communicate

Figure 39. Universal language.

with each other in languages that may be much simpler than ours but are also more universal. What is more widely understood than the warning coloration and display of a skunk? And are not the patterns of nests and burrows and trails in nature a symbolism communicating a wealth of information to those who can read it? The difference between these and human cultures is surely one of degree rather than of kind; the degree of intricacy of human symbolism is offset in part by its narrow comprehension. Only small fractions of the human species understand any one language.

Those who hold this high opinion of man seem to me prone to forget that they are not typical men; that more than half the human race is illiterate; that in Africa south of the Sahara,

112

where man is believed to have originated, neither the wheel nor written language has been indigenously developed; that many races of man, comprising a large segment of his population, tell a cultural story hardly more different from that of the great apes than it is from ours in North America, which we are apt to consider as typically human. Our outlook has got so far removed from other animals that we can no longer comprehend much of their language and symbolism; but to claim, on this account, that they have none, is to disgrace our ancestry. Man is unique, certainly, but no more unique than any other species that is a sole survivor of a genus and a family. As Le Gros Clark has said: 'Anatomically, *Homo sapiens* is unique among mammals only in the sense that every mammalian species is in some features unique among mammals'. In plants and other animals, differences that have not yet influenced structure more significantly than this rarely justify more than specific differentiation.

To set ourselves up on a superior plane, halfway to God, is thus not only incorrect, but, or so it seems to me, blasphemous and thoroughly dangerous. Let us first become master of our fate, agree on objectives for our own species, taking cognizance of our need for all others, before we take upon ourselves the mantle of divinity.

Detailed from Botticelli's "Mystic Nativity", showing the accurate representation of plants and animals. (Reproduced by courtesy of the Trustees, National Gallery, London.)

REFERENCES FOR FURTHER READING

It becomes daily more necessary to know where you can find facts rather than to know them. This selected list of books is intended to illuminate and support or qualify specific statements made in the text, and to provide further and fuller treatment of selected areas. Most of the titles contain further references; collectively they contain many thousands. This web of references, analogous to the food webs of plants and animals, stretches throughout the scientific literature and helps to give coherence to science. A good entrance to this web is a good start on the study of any scientific subject; a poor one may ensnare the reader.

CHAPTER 1

1. Karl Pearson, *The Grammar of Science*, 2nd Edition, Black, London, 1900.
2. T. H. Huxley, *Science and Culture, Collected Essays*, Macmillan, London, 1881.
3. Hugo Boyko, ed., *Science and the Future of Mankind, World Academy of Art and Science*, Junk, The Hague, 1961.
4. H. T. Pledge, *Science since 1500*, H. M. Stationery Office, London, 1939.
5. A. N. Whitehead, *Science and the Modern World*, Lowell Lectures 1925, Cambridge University Press, 1926.

CHAPTER 2

1. W. E. Le Gros Clark, *The Fossil Evidence for Human Evolution: An Introduction to the Study of Palaeoanthropology*, University of Chicago Press, Chicago, 1955.
2. George Wald, 'The Origin of Life', *The Physics and Chemistry of Life*, A Scientific American Book, Simon and Schuster, New York, 1955.
3. T. Dobzhansky, *The Biological Basis of Human Freedom*, Columbia University Press, New York, 1960.

4. Sir Julian Huxley, 'Clades and Grades', *Function and Taxonomic Importance* (pp. 21-22), The Systematics Association, Publ. No. 3, British Museum (Natural History), London, 1959.

5. C. D. O'Malley and J. B. de C. M. Saunders, *Leonardo da Vinci on the Human Body*, Henry Schuman, New York, 1952.

CHAPTER 3

1. L. Picken, *The Organization of cells, and other organisms*, Oxford University Press, 1960.

2. D'Arcy W. Thompson, *On Growth and Form* (2nd edition), Cambridge University Press, Cambridge, 1952.

3. Aristotle, *Historia Animalium, (384-22 B.C.), The Works of Aristotle Translated into English* (Vol. 4), Oxford University Press, Oxford, 1910.

4. F. J. Cole, *A History of Comparative Anatomy from Aristotle to the Eighteenth Century*, Macmillan, London, 1944.

5. R. Hooke, *Micrographia*, (Reprint 1961, Cramer, Weinheim), London, 1665.

CHAPTER 4

1. D. Lack, *Evolutionary Theory and Christian Belief. The Unsolved Conflict*, Methuen, London, 1957.

2. C. Darwin, *The Variation of Animals and Plants under Domestication* (2nd edition), John Murray, London, 1882.

3. C. Singer, *A Short History of Biology: A General Introduction to the Study of Living Things*, Oxford University Press, Oxford, 1931.

4. J. Maynard-Smith, *The Theory of Evolution*, Pelican A433, Penguin Books, Harmondsworth, 1958.

5. C. Darwin, *The Origin of Species by Means of Natural Selection* (6th edition), John Murray, London, 1872.

CHAPTER 5

1. W. T. Calman, *The Classification of Animals: An Introduction to Zoological Taxonomy*, Methuen, London, 1949.
2. C. Linnaeus, *Systema Naturae*, facsimile reprint (1956) of the 1st volume of the Xth Edition, 1758, British Museum (Natural History), London.
3. C. W. Sabrosky, 'How Many Insects Are There?', *Systematic Zoology* (vol. 2, pp. 31-36), 1963, and *Insects* (pp. 1-7), The Yearbook of Agriculture, 1952, U.S. Department of Agriculture, Washington, D.C.
4. Lord Rothschild, *A Classification of Living Animals*, Longmans, Green and Company, London, 1961.
5. O. Tippo, 'A Modern Classification of the Plant Kingdom', *Chronica Botanica* (vol. 7, p. 203), 1942.

CHAPTER 6

1. Fritz Went and the Editors of Life, *The Plants*, Life Nature Library, Time Incorporated, New York, 1963.
2. E. I. Rabinowitch, 'Photosynthesis', *The Physics and Chemistry of Life*, A Scientific American Book, Simon and Schuster, New York, 1955.
3. W. von Buddenbrock, *The Senses*, University of Michigan Press, Ann Arbor, 1958.
4. A. Szent-Gyorgy, 'Muscle Research', *The Physics and Chemistry of Life*, A Scientific American Book, Simon and Schuster, New York, 1955.
5. T. R. Malthus, *Population: The First Essay*, University of Michigan Press, Ann Arbor, 1960.

CHAPTER 7

1. R. Geiger, *The Climate Near the Ground*, Harvard University Press, Cambridge, Massachusetts, 1959.
2. V. C. Wynne-Edwards, *Animal Dispersion in relation to Social Behaviour*, Hafner Publishing Co., New York, 1962.
3. W. M. Wheeler, *The Social Insects, Their Origin and Evolution*, Routledge and Kegan Paul, London, 1928.

4. G. G. Simpson, C. S. Pittendrigh, and L. H. Tiffany, *Life: An Introduction to Biology*, Harcourt Brace, New York, 1957.
5. C. S. Elton, *The Ecology of Invasions by Animals and Plants*, Methuen, London, 1958.

CHAPTER 8

1. Cecil Woodham-Smith, *The Great Hunger*, Hamish Hamilton, London, 1964.
2. L. M. Peairs and R. H. Davidson, *Insect Pests of Farm, Garden and Orchard*, Wiley, New York, 1956.
3. J. A. Downes, 'The Gypsy Moth and Some Possibilities of the Control of Insects by Genetical Means', *Canadian Entomologist* (vol. 91, p. 661) 1959.
4. F. S. Bodenheimer, *Insects as Human Food*, W. Junk, The Hague, 1951.
5. H. Kalmus, *Variation and Heredity*, Routledge and Kegan Paul, London, 1957.

CHAPTER 9

1. H. Spencer, *The Principles of Biology*, Williams and Norgate, London, 1898.
2. N. W. Pirie, ed., *The Biology of Space Travel*, Symposium No. 10, Institute of Biology, London, 1961.
3. G. C. L. Bertram, 'Ethical Selection—The Supplanter of Natural Selection in Mankind', *Biological Problems Arising from the Control of Pests and Diseases* (pp. 107-12), Institute of Biology, London, 1960.
4. Lord Boyd Orr, 'World Population—the Future', *The Numbers of Man and Animals* (pp. 139-47), Institute of Biology, London, 1955.
5. K. von Frisch, *The Dancing Bees: An Account of the Life and Senses of the Honey Bee*, Methuen, London, 1954.